New Horizons!! Lessons for Liberty

Written by
Rev. Debbye Graafsma, mcc. bcpc
Rev. William Graafsma, DMin

Lessons for Liberty, ISBN 978-0-9852680-4-6

© 1996, 2013 Awakened to Grow

No portion of this book may be stored, duplicated or distributed in any manner, without prior written permission of the authors. Thank you for your integrity.

Awakened to Grow Ministries
P.O. Box 546
Indian Trail, NC 28079
704-562-2897

awakenedtogrow.com

New Horizons!! Lessons for Liberty
Personal Workbook -- Table of Contents

(short stories are indicated by an asterisk)
(insertion of audio recordings are indicated by an "@" sign)

Part One – Everyone Needs a Dad ——————————— 7
(How our Image of God Affects *everything!*)

*Creation	10
@ Lesson One – "The Heart of Abba Father"	
*The Shattered Father Image	16
The Heart of Father God	18
*Pandora's Box	27
@ Lesson Two – "Living Life in the Right Order"	
The Heart of Father God Towards You	37
@ Lesson Three – "Captivity or Bondage?"	
*The Explanation	45
The Father Has Chosen to Identify with You	48
The Son Has Chosen to Identify with You	60
Satan is Your Enemy – His Goal is to Bruise You	55
The Bruised Soul	58
Satan is Your Enemy – His Goal is to Wound You	63
*Count-Down	60
@Lesson Four – "The Generational Fruits of Fathering"	
*The Companion	69
The Ministry of the Holy Spirit	71

Part Two – Designed and Destined ——————————— 77
(Spiritual and Emotional Aspects of Healing Soul Wounds)

The Make-up of Man	78
*Condemnation	79
@Lesson Five – "Addressing the Wall of Pride"	
The Spirit of Man	85
*Kidnapped!	90
@Lesson Six – "The Problem with Pride, Deception, and Spiritual Imprinting"	
The Soul of Man	96
Qualities of the Human Soul	98
*Contemplation	102
The Reinforcement of the Wall of Pride	105

3 | Page

@Lesson Seven – "Relational Basics & the Religious Spirit Characteristics of the Reinforced Wall of Pride	111
What the Wall of Pride Looks Like	116
@Lesson Eight – "Forgiveness and Torment"	
*A New Beginning	127
The Earthly Tent of Man; the vessel; the Body	132
The Principles and Promise of Forgiveness	136
Notes Regarding Bondages	141

Part Three – Jesus is Our Joshua — 142
(Freedom from our Personal Jericho Strongholds)

The Choice	143
The Problem of the Bruised Will	146
Becoming Free from Self-Will	148
The Heart of Man	150
The Conscience of Man	157
How Do I Strengthen my Heart and Conscience?	152
How To Strengthen Your Will to Choose Abba's Way	165
"Say What?"	167
@Lesson Nine – "The Power of the Speaking Blood"	
Satan's Bruise of Rejection	171
@Lesson Ten – "How Abba Father Develops Character"	
A Second Chance at a First Choice	178
@Lesson Eleven – "My Jericho and Promised Land"	
Rejection's Supporting Players	183
*Deception!	197
What is a Broken Cistern?	199
The Steps to a Broken Sprit	202
Steps to Healing the Spirit	205
*Mourning Prophet	209
Steps to Healing the Will	210
What is Obedience?	212
*The Rebuilder	215
@Lesson Twelve – "How to Retain Transformation"	
The Principle of Restoration	217
Principles of Spiritual Liberty	220

New Horizons -- Lessons for Liberty
Introduction

To our Fellow Journeyers:

There is a progression of growth and healing. It begins the moment we open our lives to Jesus Christ. It is a journey of discovery, emotional development and spiritual maturing. It is a continually transforming, life-imparting work of the Holy Spirit. And it is He Who is at work in each of us, changing us from glory to glory, until we reflect and shine with the image of Christ Jesus -Who is the Hope of Glory!!

This journey is made in steps, taken one at a time, rather than in quantum leaps. Although events can occur in our lives, transforming the heart, and healing our perspective, it is the common day-to-day choices and events, which help us to grow.

There can be no growth without change.
    There can be no change without choice.
        There can be no choices made without the proper tools.

It is our desire that within these pages, dear reader, you will find tools for your emotional and spiritual toolbox – tools to equip you for the rest of your journey of discovery and growth in Christian Life.

And know this –

It is the call of the Heavenly Father, to every believer – especially to you ---

"I love you. There is no one who I have made just like you. Come up a little higher. I want to show you things you cannot even imagine. I want to trust you with My purposes, and with My heart!"

This workbook first began as a series of entries into Deb's prayer journal. They are the product of the progressive working of the Holy Spirit's gentle ministry in both of our lives, over a period of five years or more. In this process of growth, (we are still learning!), we have discovered that Jesus is always the Healer, the Holy Spirit is always the Comforter, and Abba Father is always on our side.

In these pages, we have sought to deal with the concepts of wounds and root/core issues, knowing this: in the midst of inner liberation and discovery, there will always be a place in the heart where the enemy must be exposed, confronted, and removed. We have found in most cases in the past 25 years of ministry, however, that a wounding serves as the source of any demonic difficulty or bondage within the life.

Thus, we have sought to deal with the process of inner freedom from this standpoint. Then, as a person's mind, will, understanding and emotions become renewed, many demonic problems are dealt with simply by reason of individual growth, and strengthening of a person's will.

In using these materials, may we suggest that you:

    1. Please care enough about your own freedom to look up each scripture reference.

    2. Please commit yourself to prayer as you read.

    3. Also, it is a good idea to keep a prayer journal, chronicling those memories and prayers, which come to mind as certain scriptures minister to your mind and soul. It will serve to encourage you in your growth and progress. It might be a good idea to also keep a spiral close at hand – in case the spaces we have provided for answers to questions draw deeper issues in your life to the surface.

    4. Whenever possible, find a close friend, or accountability partner -- someone to pray with you when you face areas of deepest difficulty.

It is our hope that these notes will enable you, and help to liberate you as you seek to become more like Jesus. Are you ready? Here we go.

"Now may the God of peace Himself sanctify you entirely,.. and may your spirit and soul and body be preserved complete, without blame at the coming of our Lord Jesus Christ. Faithful is He who calls you, and He also will bring it to pass."

"(God) Who delivered us from so great a peril of death, and will deliver us, He on whom we have set out hope. And He will yet deliver us... ..."

"But we all, with unveiled face, beholding as in a mirror the glory of the Lord, are being transformed into the same image from glory to glory, just as from the Lord, the Spirit."

(I Thessalonians. 5:23-24, II Corinthians 1:10 and 3:18)

New Horizons!! Lessons for Liberty

Part One –

"Everyone Needs A Dad"

Abba Father Doesn't Serve "Cafeteria Style!"

The heart of the Father has always been the same toward us. In Hebrews 13:8, the scripture says, "Jesus Christ the same; yesterday, today, and forever." In Malachi 3:6, we read "I am the Lord, I change not."

Did you know that Abba Father's purpose and desire has always been to bless you?

In the mid-second century, around 140AD, there lived a man named Marcion. Marcion was the son of a pastor, and lived in the vicinity of the Black Sea. In his adulthood, he became a ship-owner and moved to Rome. When he arrived in Rome, he met another man named Cerdo, who taught and believed that the God of the Old Testament was somehow different from the God and Father of the Lord Jesus. Cerdo told his students, whose company Marcion had now joined, that it was impossible to really know the God of the Old Testament. He was a harsh God, completely consumed with justice. On the other hand, the God of the new Christian faith was loving and full of grace. It was Cerdo's assertion that the Old Testament God should be avoided at all costs, and the New Testament God be embraced. Well, who wouldn't agree with that?

Marcion bought into the teaching with his whole heart. Armed with Cerdo's teachings, and a few added "revelations" of his own, he began the Marcionite church movement; a movement which very nearly destroyed the early church. By the time Marcion's false doctrine came into full view, those who attended his churches believed that the God of the Old Testament was full of wrath, had authored evil, and only had love for those of Jewish descent. Marcion rejected the entire Old Testament canon, as well as Matthew, Mark, Acts and Hebrews. He didn't accept the majority of Luke's gospel, either. The sections regarding the birth of Christ would have to go.

But what Scriptures could he use? He decided the apostle Paul's writings were acceptable, for the most part, and over a period of time, he elevated Paul to a place of idolatry. To support his erroneous doctrines, Marcion also taught that Christ had descended to earth twice --the first time to die as a sacrifice for sin, and the second time to call Paul to be His apostle. Paul, he contended, sits at the right hand of Christ. Never mind that Marcion had to take most if not all of Paul's letters out of context in order to arrive at these conclusions!! It is comforting, however, to note that after 4-5 years of Marcion's nonsense he was declared a heretic and his teachings unsound. But the damage had been done.

There are seeds of Marcionite teaching in the church at large today. How many times have you heard someone say "Well, that was the God of the old covenant!", or "Well, that was under the law!" Jesus said, "I did not come to destroy the law, but to fulfill it, for verily I say unto you, Till heaven and earth pass, one jot or one tittle shall in no wise pass from the law, till all be fulfilled. II (Matthew 5:17-18) (For example, the health laws given in the book of Leviticus were given by a loving Creator who knew how the body was made to function best, and what fuel it could best use for efficiency. Scientists are constantly confirming the truth of these laws of diet and health, and Father God gave them 4,000 years ago!)

Too many times, we allow ourselves to despise the God of the Old Testament, and joyfully receive the God of the New. In doing so, we customize the God we worship to our own specifications -- just like Marcion.

God the Father has always been the same. He has always been "merciful and gracious, slow to anger, and great in loving-kindness (mercy)" (Psalm 86:15) His desire to see all men come to salvation did not begin in the book of Matthew.

Jesus was the Lamb "slain from the earth's foundation." (Revelation 13:8) He knew Adam would sin, and He planned the way of salvation long before creation. He planned to take on the form and appearance of skin and bone, flesh and blood, so that we could see and understand the God of the Old Testament, and know that sin was never His idea --

He is a God of love.
    He is happy that you are here.
        He is excited about you. (Zephaniah 3: 17)

That means He planned you as well.

    You were born for a specific time, a specific purpose,

    and

    He has gifted you for His designs.

But let's get to know Him first.

Creation

Before anything else ever existed, God existed. (Genesis 1:1/ John 1)

Nothing that has ever been in existence, or has come into existence has done so without His creative power. He is what keeps the world from disintegrating. His order and power keep the world revolving on its axis, the solar system in orbit, the weather patterns functioning, and day-to-day life in balance with themselves. Mother Nature? No way! Father Creator --Originator, Designer, Merciful Benefactor and Gracious Creator. Outside of Him, nothing exists at all.

And He, just by being God, sets the boundary lines. (Colossians 1:16-17)

The Scriptures do not say why God decided to create a visible realm within the invisible realm. It does say He created angels --spiritual, unseen beings, to serve Him. (Psalm 148:2 and 5) Then, it says that God created man --both male and female. They were seen as one flesh and shared one common name --Adam. (Genesis 2:18-25) They were made in the image of God. (Genesis 1:27) As God is a three-fold being, so man is a three-fold being as well. And, it indicates that in this perfect state, they could see and interact with the unseen realm, clothed in only the glory of their Creator – which living in this tangible and limited atmosphere.

Father God also created a garden, green and lush, to be Adam's home. The garden's name was Eden. The Father gave to Adam the job of cultivating the plants and caring for the animals --(thinking about it, it must have been a much easier proposition than it would be today, considering that there were no thorns or thistles, (or even sweat!), to make the work difficult. (Genesis 2:8-15 and 3:18)

The Bible says that Father God would fellowship with Adam in the cool of the day in the garden. (Genesis 3:8) What a joy it must have been to share those quiet times alone with God, face-to-face and heart-to-heart!!

~~~~

But trouble was afoot.

One of the Father's angels, Lucifer by name, had decided to try to take God's place of authority. Lucifer had been created by the Father to be a spiritual being of glory, an arch-angel, "who covered". He was beautiful, with gold and precious stones as part of his outer design. The Father had anointed him and chosen him to serve on His holy mountain.

And, Just by moving around he made music, because harps were part of his form as well.

But Lucifer, whose name meant "Light-Bearer", became consumed with his own beauty. He became proud of his appearance and his abilities, and began to speak of himself in pride. Then, his pride turned

his nature against the Lord God. "I will sit enthroned on the mountain of the assembly," he said. "I will make myself like the Most High God." (Ezekiel 28:13-18/ Isaiah 14:9-15)

Imagine, a created being, a single expression of only part of God's nature, who has received a small, delegated morsel of the Creator's power, planning to overthrow the entire nature and reign of Almighty God!! Lucifer, so filled with his own pride, he actually believed his miniscule, *created* power could overcome the source of that power!

In addition, another problem presented itself to the Almighty. Lucifer's accusations and whisperings against the character of Father God had drawn a following! A company of the heavenly host had been deceived into rebelling along with him! Revelation 12:7-9 gives a powerful picture of the war that took place in the heavenly realm.

Predictably, Lucifer and his following were not strong enough to even stand their ground in their place of rebellion, much less advance and take more ground. Father God's loyal angelic host hurled them down to the earth.

Thus Lucifer, the "Light-Bearer", became the ruler of darkness. His beautiful outward form and design were stripped from him, and he took on the ugly forms of the Satanic symbols we see now. His preoccupation and disposition exposed its true nature. Whatever God the Father was, He would not be. If God was love, he would be hatred, fear, and indifference. If God was light, he would be the darkness. If God was joy, he would be sorrow and suffering. If God was a builder and restorer, He would be a destroyer and pacifist. If God was Truth, he would be the deceiver, the manipulator, the tempter.

All glory and distinction in the heavenly realm taken from him, he was cast aside. Away from the Presence and Glory he had desired to control for himself.

His rebellion was exposed. It was plain to see what he consisted of.

Yet, it made no difference in his attitude. To make matters worse, his fallen state did not mean a silent state. He continued to revile the Father, speaking evil. It seems that casting him down from his exalted angelic position did not change his intentions or remove his desire to rule in the heavenly realm.

Lucifer's name was changed to Satan, which means "adversary," or "enemy." He and his fallen following were cast down to earth --sentenced to be imprisoned, as it were, until the time presented itself that they should be judged by Father God. (Jude 6, II Peter 2:4, Matthew 25:41)

In his new form, full of rebellion and perverted spiritual power, Satan hid in the garden of Eden. He took on the form of a serpent; a speaking serpent. There he waited, plotting for an opportunity to once again try to usurp (supplant) the authority of Father God.

It is inconceivable that he really hoped to succeed and take God's throne, but it is true. And how he could deceive himself into thinking it was still possible defies even the least of sensibilities!!

~~~~~~~~~

Back on earth, the Father had provided Adam (male and female) with everything they could possibly desire. He had planted two evidences of His eternal nature as God in the center of the garden.

One, the Tree of the Knowledge of Good and Evil, held fruit that was beautiful to behold, but carried the understanding of the rebellion, which had taken place in the heavenly realm. It would taint anyone who ate of it, allowing that fruit to become part of his inner nature and person.

The second, the Tree of Life, was a picture of the eternal realm and all it has to offer. Father God, all-knowing and all-loving had also placed it there to speak of the Redemption which was to come; that Tree on which would be slain a Lamb not much more than 4,000 years or so down the road. That Life was eternal.

It had always been the Father's desire that life in Eden last forever.

Because He was God, the One who knows the end at the beginning, the Father had seen and prepared well for what was coming, long before creation.

~~~~~~~~~

One day, Adam (male and female) were walking in the garden, and came upon the Tree of the Knowledge of Good and Evil. While they were standing, looking at the fruit, they suddenly heard a voice.

"Has God said that you should not eat from any tree in the garden?"

Adam, male and female, looked at each other. Who was that? Who had spoken?

The woman answered, "From the fruit of the trees of the garden, we may eat; but from the fruit of the tree which is in the middle of the garden, God has said we should not eat it, or we will die."

Rebellion always causes death --usually a slow, poisoning, painful death,-- but death just the same. God is Spirit (John 4:24), and man was created in His image. Satan knew that if man would eat the fruit of this particular tree, his spirit would die immediately, but the death of the soul and body would be a long and painful one, during which he could inflict as much torment as his twisted heart desired.

How he hated them. Anything made in God's image, filled with His life and breath……

"You won't really die!" said the voice.

Curiosity was aroused. How could this voice say such things? Did this being know more than their Gracious Father?

They had never doubted the Father's words before.

The voice continued. "God knows that the minute you eat this fruit, you will be just like He is. (And He doesn't want that to happen!) You will know as much as He does. You will know what is good, and what is evil!!"

Adam, male and female, silent, stood next to the Tree.
Could this be true?

They were transfixed.

The woman thought. It does *look* good. And.... everything Father has made has tasted as good as it has looked.

She stopped and looked around. Her thoughts began to race.

"I will be more like God.
        I'll know as much, maybe more than He does -- --
                and He won't have to help me

                        --I'll have done it on my own!

The woman reached out – thinking it was the right thing to do – and picked it. (After all, the Father hadn't said not to pick it! Or had He? She couldn't remember.....)

Then she opened her mouth.

Satan held his breath. He was only two steps away from throne!!

She took a bite.

Satan crossed his fingers, and looked at the man. Just one more step before he could legally claim the authority he so badly craved!

He could feel the energy surging through his demented frame already! He laughed inwardly in anticipation. He would be ruler of the world!! It would be his legal right to do whatever He wanted! Triumph at last!

And the Father wouldn't be able to stop Him.

He had out maneuvered God.

Well, at least for now.

The woman swallowed --hard. Then she handed the fruit to the man.

The man looked at her. Then he looked at the fruit. His thoughts were racing now, as well. He didn't want to be left out. She had already eaten. All right, so the Father had said not to.

But Father wasn't here just now, so it really wouldn't matter. Hadn't He created them to be one?

The man didn't want to be left behind. She had a different look out of her eye. Had the fruit done that?

She was waiting.

After all, they were one. He had been created first, and

After all…. This voice was so informed --and intelligent!!

Besides, what the Father couldn't see wouldn't matter –
What could happen?...

The man reached out --not caring it was wrong, with alarm bells and the mournful wails of Heaven ringing deep inside --

and willfully,

SINfully,

SELFishly took the fruit.

And then, knowing exactly what he was doing, he took a bite, and swallowed -.

very hard.

And, just at that moment, in the co-existent, unseen realm –

Death walked through the door they had opened.

And from that time on, Death began to rule in the realm of physical reality.

(I Tim 2: 13-14, Genesis 3:1-24)

> **Please listen to the first CD, utilizing your notebook, for Session One**
>
> **"The Heart of Abba Father"**
> **before you move ahead**

Notes:

The Shattered Father Image

How would you describe a sunrise to someone who had never seen one? What if they had only seen the moon rising?

You would begin with their current understanding.

You would say --"It's like the moonrise, but its better."

You would say --"Imagine no darkness in the sky. That's what it is like! You've got to experience one. It's so awesome!!"

And what if the thought of the light-- the thought of what they understood to be true, but the idea that there would be more of it, scared them? What would you do if they resisted the idea?

In the heart of every person is the need for the bestowment of blessing from a father image. It was a need created by Father God.

It has always been His intention to meet that need --in every way.

Satan, the fallen and rebellious, seeks to distort that image in every life, through any method possible; anything to destroy the image of Father God; anything to cause a person to reject the Only Answer to their pain.

For this reason, God the Heavenly Father created earthly fathers. Our earthly fathers were given to us to be a tangible and touchable representation of the nature of Father God. But if an earthly father has no understanding of Father God --if he has no road map --how can he point the way for the lives of his children?

What an impossible task!

Yet, in every life, the father image is formed during childhood. It is the basis for our adult perceptions and understandings. It acts as the filter through which responses are given. It is the pattern for our own behavior as we grow. Interpreted through the actions of our mother, it imprints us with our understanding of our own value and place on the planet.

> It is the beginning place of our own identity.
> It is also the place where we learn to bond with other human beings.

As a person grows into adulthood, their perceptions and understandings of any and all authority figures are also filtered through the father image. A person learns to trust authority, or to distrust authority; develop the habit of obedience, or become defensive and reclusive. A person will perceive acceptance and become secure, or they retreat into an inner shell, and learn the "safety nets" and person justification mechanisms of fear, pride and rejection.

As a result, all intimate relationships in the person's life, whether friendship or marital, can go no further than the degree of unity and relationship (bonding) gained with the person's earthly father.

Then -- A person comes to Christ, and their spirit is reborn.

Always, in our ministry experience, there comes a point in their growth and development, when the two images must become separate. It usually happens after salvation; sometimes long after. Many times, I person will feel the need to continue living with the pain they have experienced prior to coming to Christ, without allowing the Lord Jesus to touch and heal the places wounded so deeply in early years of development.

In each person, the earthly father image has become the picture of the ultimate authority as well; meaning, what is understood to be true is transferred to become the explanation of their Heavenly Father. For example, if earthly dad was an angry man who expected perfection, a person might believe Father God has the same character. If earthly dad was too busy to be available for them, they seem to have a hard time believing that Father God will listen when they pray. Why should they think anything else?

All they have seen is the moonrise.

It is vitally important, as a basis for our spiritual and emotional health and growth, that we understand just exactly who we are dealing with when we come to Father God.

What is His character? What does He really feel about us?

> He has given us His Word. Are we willing to believe it is true?
>
> He has asked us to trust Him. Some of us find that difficult to do.
> We never were able to trust authority before. Will He take care of us? Will He let us fall?
>
> Are we truly important to Him? Does He really love us?
>
> And, after all, what is love, anyway?
>
> Look at it this way … …

> *He has given us His Son. (And in Him are all things pertaining to life and godliness)*

The Heart of Father God

Who is He? What is He like?

"The Lord is gracious and merciful; slow to anger and great in loving-kindness The Lord is good to all, and His mercies are over all His works." II Psalm 145:8-9

1. He is a Triune (three-part) Being   Galatians 4:4-6
(Three distinct Persons, yet unified in identity)

    a. The Father (Originator)   Romans 1:7
    --all powerful   Jeremiah 32: 17 and 27
    --all knowing   I John 3:20
                                              Hebrews 4:13

What does this tell you about His strength and ability to help you?

_____

_____

    b. Jesus, the Son (Physical example)   Romans 1:7
     --the touchable and tangible Account,   Colossians 1:12-18
    or Picture of the Father
    (Greek --Logos)
                                         John 1: 1-5
                                         John 1:17-18

What do you understand about Jesus' position in relation to the Father? (He was present at Creation, but also, it is important that we understand as believers that Jesus Christ is God, and that He came in the form of flesh)

_____

_____

_____

_____

c. The Holy Spirit (Invisible Presence of His nature)
    --omni-present --He is everywhere

Ephesians 4:30
Psalm 139:7-12

Think of the places when you feel most alone. Is the Presence of Father God with you? List them here.

_____

_____

2. He is the Creator of everything seen and unseen

Colossians 1: 15-17

Do you understand that He has control of everything? What things do you wish you could give Him control over in your own life?

_____

_____

3. He is Spirit (not a spirit *being,* but He *is* spirit)

John 4:24

Does His essence exist everywhere?

_____

4. He is good

Psalm 34:8

Does the ability to be evil even exist within His nature?

_____

5. He is stronger than anything.

Luke 1:37
Romans 8:31

Is there anything He can be prevented from doing?

6. He is a man of war --a warrior   Exodus 15:3
                                         II Chronicles 20: 17

Will He fight for you?

---

7. He is the Essence of light   I John 1:5
                                         Revelation 21:23

Are there shadows, or dark places (places which cause terror) within His character?

(It is important that we realize that if Father God is Light, and is the Father of Light, that His personality and character have no "dark side". He knows everything, sees everything, and always ministers to His children those things, which bring Life.)

8. He separated the light from the darkness   Genesis 1: 1-4

He called the light "good". He separated it from the darkness. Can He do the same creative miracle within your life? List two areas in which you feel this need.

---

9. He has manifested Himself
    a. in a cloud   Exodus 34:5-7
    b. his voice sounds like thunder   Revelation 14:2
    c. his voice sounds like many waters   Revelation 1:12-18
    d. As Jesus Christ, the provision for
       our freedom from darkness   Ephesians 2:1-6
                                                   I Peter 2:8-9
                                                   John 14:6

Do these scriptures show that He is willing to allow Himself to be seen and that He wants us to understand His heart as well as His ways?

10. He is glorious in holiness,   Exodus 15: 11
    invoking awe, and doing wonders

Holiness is part of His character. It is not a legalistic demand which He makes of Himself. Because of this nature, there is no lack of glory in what He accomplishes in and for His children. Based upon your own experiences --In what way does this observation differ from your own heart's understanding of authority figures?

_____

11. He is merciful and full of grace   Psalm 86:15

Think of the representation of Father God. How do you picture Him? (For example, is He waiting for you to fail so He can punish you? Are His judgments harsh? Is He angry? Do you feel you must attain perfection for receive His attention?)

Compare that image with what the Word of God says in the above scripture. What differences do you see between the two?

_____

_____

12. He designed and planned the   James 1:17
idea of everything good and perfect

What does this scripture say about the gifts Father God gives us?

_____

Does He change His mind about us?

_____

13. He designed and planned the idea of faith   Hebrews 12:2

Does He want you to have the ability to believe?

_____

14. His character does not vary.
He is consistent and does not change

Acts 10:34
Hebrews 13:8
James 1:11

Does He have favorite children who are blessed more than others? --- According to Scripture, can we always expect Him to receive us in the same way? (Do His moods <u>change?</u>)

_____

15. He cannot lie

Hebrews 6: 18
Numbers 23:19

These scriptures indicate that the tendency to lying is part of the fleshly nature, and does not exist within the nature of Father God? Since He never lies, can you trust His Word to guide you? List an area in which you need to learn to trust Him here.

_____

_____

16. He always keeps His promises

Numbers 23:19

Has an authority figure ever made a promise and not kept it in your experience? Has that damaged your ability to believe? This scripture says that God the Father ALWAYS keeps His promises! What promises have you struggled to believe from the Word of God for your own life? Is it possible that Father God would honor those promises for you?

_____

_____

17. He hates sin and cannot be tempted by it

Proverbs 6:16-19 (verses 12-15 also)

These things are directly opposed to the nature of Father God. They do not exist within His being. For this reason, when a person practices these things, they are living their lives outside of His blessing and protection. Have any of these attitudes and practices been directed toward you from an earthly authority figure? How has that confused your image of Father God?

_____

18. He is faithful   I Corinthians 1:9
                                                               Hebrews 10:23

Faithfulness is a description of the character of Father God. It means that He will always continue to do what He has done in the past, and that He will always be there. What needs do you see in your own life for faithfulness on the part of an authority figure?

_____

_____

19. He is just; and Justice establishes His
authority as God   Psalm 89:14

Just: "Upright, honest. Fair and impartial. Merited or deserved. A valid, correct, and legitimate judgment. (Root word of Justification). (Doubleday)

Father God gives correct and honest assessments of people and situations. That is the basis for His authority to be God. He keeps accounts. Have you struggled with accepting this image of Him because of the failure of earthly authority figures to validate your basic needs? What areas do you see now that you trust to be released to Him?

_____

_____

20. He is righteous; and Righteousness establishes
His authority as God

Lovingkindness (mercy) and truth explain Him   Psalm 89: 14
before He comes

Father God is blameless in His character. He is the Blesser, not the curser --(see John 10:10). How does this change your image of who you understood Him to be?

_____

_____

21. He is forgiving   I John 1:9
                                   Isaiah 43:25
                                   Isaiah 55:7
                                   Jeremiah 31:34

Forgive: *"To grant pardon for, or remission of To cease to blame or feel resentment against. To remit a debt. II (Doubleday)*

Did you know that He forgives us when we ask Him? (We don't have to beg!!)

Are there areas in your life, needing His forgiveness?

Use this paper to confess them. Write out a short prayer here.

_____

_____

_____

_____

_____

_____

22. He chooses to forget what He forgives   Psalm 103:12
                                              Isaiah 43:25-26

How far is the east from the west? Do they ever meet? When we ask forgiveness, there are no strings attached. He washes our failures and sins from us, and wants to help us to become new in behavior and heart --never to sin in the same way again. What new aspects of Father God's character have you discovered through this lesson? Please list them here.

_____

_____

23. He is the essence of unconditional love   I John 4:7-8

Does Father God's love toward you change according to your successes and failures in living life? Is He selective --accepting some and rejecting others?

_____

24. The Evidences of His Nature   Galatians 5:22-23

    a. *Love* -- Greek --"agape" (Unconditional, limitless love)
    b. *Joy* -- Greek --"chara" (joy, gladness)
    c. *Peace* -- Greek --"eirene" (security, safety, prosperity -because peace and harmony make and keep things safe and prosperous)
    d. *Patience* -- Greek -"makrothumia" (longsuffering, steadfastness, perseverance, slowness in avenging wrongs)
    e. *Kindness* -- Greek --"chrestotes" (moral goodness, integrity, benignity)
    f. *Goodness* -- Greek -"agathosune" (uprightness of heart and life, coupled with kindness)
    g. *Faithfulness* --Greek --"pistis" (conviction of the truth, fidelity, faithfulness, the character of one who can be relied upon and trusted)
    h. *Gentleness* -- Greek --"praotes" (gentleness, mildness, meekness)
    i. *Self-Control* -- Greek --"egkrateia" (temperance, the virtue of one who masters his desires and passions, especially those sensual appetites which appeal to the carnal man)

These elements of His character not only explain who He is, but they also describe how He deals with us as His children. He is always gentle, always faithful, always loving without condition upon that love. Moreover, because He comes to live inside our hearts when we give our lives to Him, He will express His nature and character through us, as we yield to His dealings within us. List here those areas, which seem particularly painful when yielding to Him.

_____

25. He is honorable 　　　　　　　　　　　Psalm 111:3

There is nothing in His character, which does not invoke respect and admiration. Are there ways in which you lost respect for the authority figures you have known? List the things, which have opened the door to suspicion and mistrust of authority here.

_____

_____

26. He has made his wonderful works to　　　Psalm 111:4-10
　　　　be remembered　　　　　　　　　　Jeremiah 29:11-13

Father God wants you to be constantly reminded that His plans for your life are for good, and not for evil. What does this scripture say He has provided as part of His works?

_____

_____

27. His desire is to walk among us　　　　　Leviticus 26: 11-12
　　　　　　　　　　　　　　　　　　　　　Romans 8:31

Does your Heavenly Father want to spend time with you?

_____

_____

28. He wants everyone to experience salvation,　　I Timothy 2:3-4
　　　　coming to the knowledge of the Truth

Is it even possible that all of Father God's goodness and blessings are for everyone except you? Write out verse four here.

_____

_____

Pandora's Box

"Adam." A few seconds of silence followed.

"Adam." In the cool of the day, God the Father was calling.

Adam (male and female) weren't sure if it was really Him. After all, as soon as the fruit was swallowed, each had experienced something new; something terrible; something wrong.

There had always been Light before. There had always been Music before. There had always been the ability to hear, see and feel those glorious beings…. So powerful, so majestic….

Suddenly the peace had been broken. A new substance had filled them. Dark and heavy in its atmosphere, it carried with it a new sense of something almost tangible.

Pain.

Something wonderful and glorious; something full of the reality of the eternal realm --

had Died.

They could feel it.

What did that mean? They wondered.

"Adam."

It was not a physically audible voice… not to the man and woman…. Not any longer. Now, it was as though they could hear Him, but through a tunnel; unfocused, unclear, confused with other noises and babble that they had never been aware of before. The fellowship they had shared to that point had been an inward and deeply satisfying friendship. But they could sense it would no longer be this way –

What had they done? Why had they listened?

"Adam." Never before had He needed to pursue Adam.

In order to heal His creation, Abba Father made Himself known on the physical level. He stepped in physical form into the visible realm. How He longed to draw them to His heart. But now, rather than hearing and understanding from deep within their being, from the spiritual part of them that resonated with His glory, the man and the woman would have to fight through fear, accusation and confusion.

Now, rather than being led by their spirits, Adam would be ruled by their will.

Looking ahead, Abba could see – the will to choose well, would be bruised as well.

****

Adam, (male and female), looked at each other. Somewhere deep inside, suddenly a shadow had fallen upon them. Was it darker outside?

"I can't hear Father." The man looked down, and realized he was still holding the fruit in his hand. "Something ..." he looked around. "Something's wrong!" He dropped the fruit.

"And whose fault is that?"

She spoke. However, the voice was no longer gentle. It had developed a harsh sound. She blinked in surprise, hearing its edge. "I'm cold."

The man slapped a small insect, which was beginning to bore into his flesh.

"I don't feel right. We didn't do what the Father told us. We ate that fruit. And, now I .... ." His voice trailed off. He held his head in his hands. The brilliant mind, which had named each of the animals, and kept track of each plant's growth record, now, could not even form the words to express what was happening inside his own heart.

"I know one thing! I'm going to do something about this. I'm not walking around without anything to wear. Look at me! I'm naked! And I'm cold." She spoke again, the tone of accusation and anger wearing thinly at the surface.

"Yes, I know you are," he sighed. "But that's the point, isn't it? We didn't even know it before. All that mattered was the Father. We were clothed in His glory, and He surrounded us, but now... Now we are naked."

He paused, thinking." I took that fruit from you. I knew it was wrong, and it killed that part of me inside --that part that clothed me in glory; His glory… That must be why I can't hear Him now."

She thought for a moment and then answered. "I felt it too. I'm sorry."

"I know. So am I."

The woman walked over to a small fig tree and began pulling off its leaves, one at a time. The man watched her for a short time, and then joined her in the first tedious task they had ever undertaken. They made coverings for themselves. In the middle of the job, they heard a Voice, a familiar, yet physically audible Voice, from deep within the garden.

"Adam."

They looked at each other, and hurried to finish their coverings. Coverings would mask their vulnerable, naked need from the eyes of Abba Father God.

The Voice came again.

"Adam."

They whispered. They had never felt a need to whisper before.

"Hurry! He's coming. I don't want Him to see me like this."

"What do you think I'm doing? I'm doing the best I can!"

"Adam." His Voice was closer now. They could hear footsteps on the leaves.

The whispers continued. "Move. Hide over there."

"Where?"

"Behind that big oak tree." They crept stealthily over the soft grass, stealing a hidden spot where they thought their Father wouldn't find them.

But you know -- The Father wasn't looking for Adam in order to dole out a punishment.

"Where are you?" He called. It was a saddened question. The Father could see them. He knew exactly where they were hidden. But in order to help Adam, there had to be a reckoning – a facing and admission of what had gone wrong.

So the Fruit had stolen that great a part of them already, had it?

Crouching in the darkness, the man and the woman both knew deep within that the only way to make this dark and terrible heaviness go away, was to tell Him.

Just tell Him.

They wanted to. But it didn't seem to be that simple. A great battle was taking place within man. This was unfamiliar! Why was it suddenly so difficult to talk to Abba Father? The seconds ticked by. The pressure mounted within the man's heart. He could feel his heart beating like a mighty thunder in his ears.

He whispered to himself, practicing. "I was afraid of You… so I hid… we… we hid."

He licked his lips and spoke a little louder. His throat felt dry and constricted. He struggled to get the words out. Something inside his stomach was churning with fear.

"I heard You in the garden and afraid because I was naked. So I hid myself."

Adam (male and female), had still not moved out into full view,

Abba Father waited. He wanted to be able to help Adam. He couldn't change the consequences of the weights and measures which had been put into action, but He could help him. How dare Satan trespass on this aspect of creation! The rebellion continued! This entire mechanism had been set in motion by a choice….. just one choice. So, in order for the Father to be able to help Adam, Adam had to choose to come willingly to the Father.

Abba would not force Him to choose. And watching his fallen son, the Father saw every other son and daughter of Adam still waiting in his loins to step on to the planet. They would have to choose willingly s well.

Abba spoke. He did not speak to the Fear. That was the adversary's method of ruling – intimidating, controlling, accusing…… No, Abba spoke to the partial knowledge Adam had received.

"Who told you that you were naked?" Adam needed to see the source of this new imprinting in his soul.

And, even though no response was voiced, a response was made.

                The response was Silence – which led to Distance.

Abba Father waited for an answer. "Have you eaten the fruit that I told you not to eat?"

****

Satan, still sitting inside the tree of the Knowledge of Good and Evil, began to chuckle to himself. There was no way out for them now. This was delicious! His mouth watered in anticipation. The Garden would be his to rule! The earth was his to rule!! The man and the woman would have to do what he told them to do. He could drive them!! He could make them try to reach unattainable goals!!

He could sit back and watch them destroy themselves trying to please each other!! Better still, he could bolster Selfishness in their hearts. That would cause them to hurt and abuse each other. Blame would be a still easier device to use.

Oh it was going to be a grand time!

****

Abba Father watched His creation struggle with the seeds of Death they had ingested.

The man and the woman had no idea on a conscious level of the terrible forces they had unleashed by their actions. For the first time since drawing breath, deep within, they each experienced anguish and cried out. It was a wrenching, eye-opening sob of regret.

It was the guilt-ridden wail of a poisoned soul.

"Help us! We want to go back to the way it was! We want to live again! Please make life better than this! There must be more to look forward to!"

It was not a physically audible scream, but in the ears of Abba Father, it was the loudest noise ever heard.

Silence continued. Adam (male and female) looked at each other. Could they admit to Him they had eaten the fruit? What would He do to them?

The man made a choice. He looked away from her and spoke. "It was the woman's fault. You know, the one *You* gave me. She did it. She gave me the fruit to eat, and I ate it."

The Father had been accused before. He had seen this nature before --in the heavens --in a spiritual dimension. He knew its source, Nor was He surprised. He had expected this,

And for just a second, --no, a split-millisecond, He looked beyond the newly hung veil of Time, to a hill on the outskirts of a city called Jerusalem. He looked ahead to the Cross.

He looked at the woman. "What have you done?"

She began to cry. Deep sobs broke out from within the delicate, feminine expression He had created. No longer joyous and innocent, but now broken and full of heaviness, she answered, pointing to the tree of Knowledge.

"It was the serpent's fault. He made me think it was what You wanted me to do. And I did it. I didn't mean to. It's not all my fault. He *made* me do it. I ate it."

This side of the adversary's nature was also not new to the eyes of the Father. For, when Lucifer had been stripped of his glory, he had authored this system of pity and blame-shifting.

Before another word could be said, the all-seeing eyes of Abba Father looked inside the very nature of the tree of the Knowledge of Good and Evil. And Satan, the ruler of darkness, formerly Lucifer the "Light-Bearer," heard the Voice which had spoken his existence and later his ex-communication from the heavens.

He cowered in fear. He shrunk down, trying to escape the awesome Power that shot towards him like a bolt of lightning. The reality of his puny existence was about to be exposed to the man and the woman.

"You are cursed, more than every beast of the field. The form you have taken will crawl on its belly and eat dust all its days. I will allow hostility to rule between you and the woman. But beware! There will come a day when seed from her loins will crush you, even though you bruise that seed on His heel."

Satan slithered from the Garden as fast as he could.

The Voice continued. But the tone changed to tenderness as He gazed upon the woman. These two had no idea of what they had done to the Paradise He had planned for them. He spoke her.

"Things have changed, you know, my daughter. Anything birthed through your life will now come forth in the midst of pain. Because of this, that pain will be greatly multiplied now, because of your choice to sin. And you will have a desire to control your husband – that will your method of hiding your pain. And now, he will hide his weaknesses as well – he will seek to become a ruler over you. His pride will be his folly."

The woman continued to weep; not this; not *more* pain; *more* sorrow. Wasn't He going to fix things? How could she live like this?

The Father looked upon the man. His heart grieved; grieved from its core. The plans would have to be delayed, that was all…..

> And this one. This comparatively small, un-replaceable, individual segment of His creation was now be sentenced to live with a poisoned soul.

But in the midst of grief.. …the Father found joy.

It was a wonderful thing. And it spoke hope for millions of generations to come.

In the midst of their pain, the man and the woman had responded to His call. They had been honest with Him. They were penitent. They had confessed the sin of their soul. The doorway to Healing had opened!!

The Father thought.

Because the tree had grown from the ground, and because Adam had eaten of it -- causing sin to begin its ruler-ship, the ground would have to be cursed as well as the serpent. In addition, He would explain to Adam the reason for the hardships to come. He spoke.

> "The ground is cursed because of what you have done here.
> You will work with sorrow all of your life.
>
> It will now grow thorns and thistles for you,
> Even when you are seeking to grow crops.
>
> Your body will sweat now,
> Even when you are enjoying the fruit of your labors.
>
> And because you were made from the dust,
> When your body dies, it will go back to being dust."

Adam (the man), blinked back the tears and fell at the Father's feet. Eve (the woman), reached out for consolation. The Father wept over them. He held them. His heart longed to remove the wounds and stains of their sin. He longed to renew the spirit-life within them.

He spoke to them tenderly. He lifted up their heads. He smiled through His sadness.

"We can still be together, you know. But it will be harder now --for you."

And, then,
    because the first, once- perfect Adam had chosen Self before obedience,
    and sin had entered his heart,

    because Abba Father would again enter the tangible realm in a tangible form, but that time
    as, the Last Adam, perfect and without sin;

    because He would come in the form of flesh and blood, and NOT give in to the tempting serpent,

    because the human spirit had died to all things good and eternal,
    and would have to be re-born into the spiritual and perfect realm,

    because the only physical picture of Life was now the blood,
    which continually circulated --hidden within man's body,
    keeping the works of death from overtaking his greatly reduced life --

and

    because an innocent life, an animal's life, offered, could serve as a temporary substitute
    for the Perfect, Sinless, One until the proper time,

    The Father made the first sacrifice for sin.

    He covered His creation.

    Then, He sent them, sadly, from the former Paradise called Eden.

    Looking at the tree of Life, Abba Father firmly and gently took action. Calling one of the cherubim --one of the loyal angels who had stood with Him and defended the Throne during the rebellion, He spoke.

"Station yourself here. The man knows what we know now; but he has not completely chosen the side on which he will stand. He must choose. He must master his will."

"I have sent him from the Garden. His human nature now feels the draw toward sin; and I must set a boundary for that sin. If the man and the woman take and eat the fruit of the tree of Life, he will live forever. We will not allow sin to live forever."

The angel, a glorious and majestic being, nodded, and took up his post. He stood by the Tree to guard the path leading to its fruit. Abba Father gave him a sword; a flaming sword, which turned in every direction.

From that point onward, sin would be limited in its operation. Satan, though he had operated in a limited sphere before, would know more limits in regard to his dealings with man. He would now have to give a periodic accounting of his doings on the earth. Moreover, Abba Father would give man His laws, which would enable him to see the power of Satan's law of sin and death.

(Job 1:6-7/2:1/ Genesis 3:14-15/Revelation 21:27/ Romans 14:12)

John 1:18 says that "no man has seen God at any time, but the only begotten God, who is in the bosom of the Father *(that's Jesus),* He has explained Him." That means: when Father God took on the physical realm to find the man and woman in their sin, *Jesus* found them. *Jesus* covered them. *Jesus* wept with them.

> He is the explanation of the Father.

He is also the only way to the Tree of Life. No one can live forever without coming through Jesus first. In Genesis 3:24, the cherubim stood with the flaming Sword which turned in every direction. It was a spiritual Sword. Ephesians 6: 17 says that the Sword of the Spirit is the Word of God.

(John 1:1-2, Revelation 1:11-18)

> Jesus Christ is that Word.

> Jesus Christ is the only Way back into Paradise.

> **Please listen to the second CD, utilizing your notebook, for Session Two**
>
> **"Living Life in the Right Order"**
> **before you move ahead**

Notes:

The Heart of Father God Towards You

"What then shall we say to these things? If God be for us, who can be against us?" Romans 8:31

1. He called you to accomplish a given purpose   Isaiah 49: 1 and 5
when you were still inside your mother's womb.
He designed you to be His arrow (prepared, aimed
and targeted at a specific time for a strategic
purpose within your own generation)

Did you know that Father God, your Creator, made you as a special custom-fit design? You are His "*poema*", or workmanship, created for good works. Write out Ephesians 2:10 here, using the words "I" and "me", rather than "us" and "we".

_____

_____

2. You were not hidden from Him when you were   Psalm 139:13-16
forming in your mother's womb. He knew all
about your life. He numbered the days of your
life before you were born.

What conceptions about your life, and your life's purpose does this Scripture confront and bring to light?

_____

_____

3. He wants to bless you and make your name great   Genesis 12:1-3
He wants to make you a blessing. He wants to bless   Galatians 3:7-9
those who bless you and curse those who curse you.

Father God is an authority figure who will defend you against all enemies. No matter how you have been failed by an earthly authority figure in this area of your life, write here those areas in which you know you need to trust Father God to defend and keep you.

_____

4. He wants to pardon all your iniquities　　　　　　　　　　Psalm 103:3-5 and 10
*(inherited weaknesses and tendencies to sin,
Guilt which has been stored up from one
generation to another).* He wants to heal all
of your diseases. He wants to redeem
(make new) your life, pulling you from the pit.
He wants to crown your life with loving-kindness
and compassion. He wants to satisfy your years
with good things. He wants to renew your youth
(give you strength in your later years).

What is the overwhelming provision of Father God according to these verses? Are you important to Him? Is He aware of your circumstances? In what ways do these scriptures confront your earthly understanding of a father figure?

_____

_____

5. He doesn't deal with us according to our　　　　　　　　Psalm 103:10
sins. (That means we don't get what we deserve –
That's GRACE!)

Is our Heavenly Father waiting to punish us when we fail? _____

6. There is no limit to His loving-kindness　　　　　　　　Psalm 103: 11 and 17
(that is --His gentle and steadfast mercy) towards
us.

Is He always willing to accept us and forgive us, when we repent and confess our sin?

_____

7. He wants to make your paths straight.　　　　　　　　Proverbs 3:5-6

Is He able to make good come from bad? Will He help us and teach us so that we don't <u>fail?</u> (See Romans 8:28)

_____

8. He wants to give the Holy Spirit to those who ask Him. He gives good gifts.
    Luke 11:9-13
    James 1:11

What gifts have you been afraid to ask for from you Heavenly Father? Why?

_____

_____

9. He wants to be your strength when you are weak.
    Exodus 15:2
    II Corinthians 12:9

In what ways do you see a different understanding of Father God and His love for you than you have known before? Explain.

_____

_____

10. He wants you to live forever
    John 3:14-18
    II Peter 3:9
    John 8:23,24

Is Father God glad that you are here? Did He plan your existence? _____

11. He wants you to see the Kingdom of God
    John 3:3
    John 6:40

Does He want to spend time with you? _____

Write out a short description of the new pictures of Abba Father that have become real to you so far in this study. In what ways is He different from the concept you have had of Him in your life until now?

_____

_____

12. He wants His blessings to overtake you. He wants to bless you in the city, and bless you in the country. He wants to bless your children, and all the animals you possess. He wants to bless your food situation. He wants to bless you when you go out and when you come in. He wants to cause your enemies to be defeated before you, fleeing in seven different directions. He wants to bless everything you set your hand to do. He wants to establish you, and prosper you. He wants to bless you so that you are a lender and not a borrower. He wants to make you the head and not the tail. He wants to bless you so that you are on top in every situation.

Deuteronomy 28:1-13

What does this Scripture teach you about His nature toward you? Has he designed you to fail?

_____

What is the condition for success in life, according to these verses?

_____

Since Father God's Word is true, and He always keeps His promises, and He does not practice favoritism, can you believe that all of these blessings can be yours when you choose to obey Him?

_____

What, or who, seeks to keep you from obeying His Word? _____

What, or who, seeks to keep you from trusting Father God with your heart so that you will succeed?

_____

13. He wants you to have an *abundant* life   John 10:10
"abundant" --Greek "perissos" (beyond measure,
much more than all, superior, more remarkable
and excellent than you've ever known before)

What is abundant life, in your perspective? Is it just possessions and starns? Or does it go beyond that, into abundant blessings of a healthy soul? (See III John 3)

_____

14. He wants you to operate in the gifts of His Spirit   Acts 2:17-18

Does the promise extend to you, and to your life? _____

15. He wants to be your refuge. He will not   Psalm 9:9-10
forsake (abandon) you.   Hebrews 13:5

How long has He promised to be with you? _____

16. He wants to deliver you from all evil,   Psalm 34:17
and save you from all your enemies.   Psalm 18:1-3

Has an earthly authority figure failed you by allowing you to be subjected to evil? Have they put you in a harmful situation, and thereby bruised your ability to trust? Can you trust what Father God has said in His Word about His ability to keep you and deliver you?

_____

_____

7. He wants you to trust in Him and to be helped.   Psalm 28:7

It is important that we realize that there is no complete and lasting help outside of Father God. Only He can heal us. Are you willing *to* open your heart, and allow His love *to* touch those places which have been bruised in the past?

_____

_____

18. He has stored up His goodness for you. 	Psalm 31:20
He wants to hide you in his Presence.

19. He wants to be your Helper 	Hebrews 13:5-6

Are you willing to allow yourself to believe these attributes about Father God, in direct relation to your life?

_____

_____

20. He knows your inabilities and has pity on you. 	Psalm 103:13

Does Father God expect perfection from your life? _____

21. He wants to shine on your life like the sun, 	Psalm 84:11-12
and be your Shield. He wants to pour out grace
and glory upon you. He doesn't want to with-hold
any good things from you.

What spiritual and emotional blessings do you need to receive from your Heavenly Father?
_____

_____

22. He wants to supply all your needs. 	Philippians 4:19

What needs do yon have that you have been afraid to ask Father God to meet?
_____

_____

23. He wants to shine His countenance
(He's watching with love) upon you to light your way. 	Psalm 89:15

24. He wants to cleanse your life from all sin, 	I John 1:7
and have fellowship (intimate friendship) with you.

25. He wants you to know that He is on your side.   Psalm 118:6

Can you believe that Father God will give you the understanding and perspective you need to live your life to a fuller dimension? What new understanding of His nature do these scriptures provide for you?

_____

_____

_____

_____

26. He wants to revive (heal) your heart   Isaiah 57: 15
when you have been broken and bruised.

27. He wants write His laws into your mind,   Hebrews 8:10-12
and write them on your heart, to keep you   Psalm 119:11-12
from sin and destruction.   Proverbs 14:12/16:25

Only Heavenly Father can equip and enable you to walk free from the pain and bondage you have experienced in your life. *(Human beings are qualified, and can help you to understand why you have pain, and how to live with it --but only the One who Created you can remove it and give you a new heart.)* **Write a prayer to Him here, asking for His help, and then pray what you have written out loud.**

_____

_____

_____

_____

28. He wants to deliver you from all fear. Psalm 34:4-7
He wants to deliver you from all shame.
He wants to deliver you out of all your troubles.

29. He wants to answer your prayers, and give I John 5: 14-15
you confidence that He hears you. (He is listening)

30. He is the Restorer of your soul. Psalm 23:3

31. He wants you to be unafraid of His Presence, Galatians 4:4-7
and to come to Him as his little child. Romans 8:15-16
  Hebrews 4: 16
  Matthew 18:1-4

32. To this point, draw a comparison chart from your own personal life experience.

My Abba Father	My Earthly Father
characteristics	comparative characteristics
1.	1.
2.	2.
3.	3.
4.	4.
5.	5.
6.	6.
7.	7.
8.	8.
9.	9.
10.	10.

**Please listen to the third CD, utilizing your notebook, for Session Three
"Generational Fortresses: Captivity or Bondage?"
before you move ahead**

Notes:

The Explanation

It was a warm and sunny day. Seven-year old Luis was playing outside in the grass behind his home. He loved to play outside. Especially when the sun was out. It was fun.

Bordering the property was a brick wall, which served as a protection from the street traffic just beyond the yard. There was a sidewalk between the wall and the street, and during the afternoons on some days, the young boy enjoyed perching on the top of the wall and watching the happenings around him. Today was such a day.

There were so many things to see: the women walking by with their shopping bags; the children walking to the store; the men with the cement truck, repairing a hole in the road; the woman with the baby stroller. Than came the ice cream truck, and the huge bus with all the passengers. There was even a dog, with his head sticking out of a window!

Munching on an apple, Luis imagined a parade --a parade where he could march in the center and play the
big bass drum! !

In the middle of his reverie, Luis looked down.

An ant was crawling along the front of the wall. It was carrying a crumb of bread which was bigger than its entire body. "How do they do that?" Luis thought to himself. Jumping down onto the sidewalk, he decided to follow the ant and watch it find its way home. "I wonder where it lives," he questioned.

But the ant crawled to the end of the wall, and then turned around, and retraced its path to the other end of the bricks. It seemed to be looking for something. Several times, the insect followed the same pattern. "It can't find the crack in the wall it came through," Luis concluded. The boy went inside the house to find his toy magnifying glass. Perhaps *he* could find the crack in the wall.

The ant was still crawling and still carrying the burden of the breadcrumb.

Like a little detective, Luis searched the wall inch by inch for over an hour until he found the crack in the wall, which looked as though it might have been the little insect's original entrance to the street. How could he get the ant to go through the hole? An idea occurred to the little boy. He ran inside the yard to find a fallen branch from one of the trees in the yard.

If he could persuade the ant to climb onto the stick, he could show it where the crack in the wall was.

Perfect!!

But it didn't work. The ant refused to climb onto the stick. To make matters worse, it's pace was slowing now. Luis was frustrated.

When his father came home from work, Luis asked for help. Taking his father by the hand, they walked out to the sidewalk. The ant was still there, but it was just standing now, exhausted, its energy spent. Innumerable trips back and forth in front of the wall had brought it to the end of its tiny reserve of reliance. It was still carrying the burden of the crumb.

"How can I help the ant, Daddy?" Luis looked up into his father's eyes.

"You have to show it where the crack in the wall is, son."

"I tried that. I even used a stick. It wouldn't climb up on it."

"It didn't understand. I guess the ant world is a little different than our world." The father spoke gently now.

"If I could speak his language, I could tell him."

The father sought to comfort his son. "It would take more than that, Luis. You would have to become an ant, learn to live in his world, and then you could tell him. But you would have to get him to trust you, to listen to you --and then follow you."

Sound familiar?

Most people live with walls; walls within the soul. Walls built to protect and guard the human identity from pain. Its funny, but contrary to popular belief, no one has ever built a wall to protect their strengths. We all seek to protect the places where we are weakest, don't we? Some are walls we build ourselves; and some are built for us, constructed before we were born by our family structure, our ethnicity, our culture.

Perhaps your walls were made before you even knew how to hold a brick -- and perhaps your identity was scarred through the carelessness and selfishness of other people --

Most people in the world are like the ant. They spend a lifetime traveling from one end of the wall to the other, looking for the path past the pain. They seek to find a way to avoid dealing with it – they just try to get around it somehow – or just keep on hoping and wishing that it will go away on its own. The problem is, that within every heart is the need and hunger for love – Real love. Love that brings emotional health and freedom.

It is a fact that no one can be completely free, or "real," or "at home" without getting through the wall. And innately, we each perceive it. There is a place --somewhere --where we each can discover who we were really created to be. There has to be a someone --somewhere --who can make us really happy.

The problem is that "somewhere" doesn't exist on the outside the wall.

And only Father God, the Creator, knows who he created each of us to become. He is the only one who knows where we belong, and how we will be truly happy.

Consider this: If His image is distorted in our lives --and we are afraid to seek Him -- or we think He is always looking for perfection is us –
                  or we assume He is angry --
                                or we think He doesn't care --

How can He speak into our lives?

That is what the life of Jesus was all about. In John 6:30, Jesus said, "The Father and I are one." Father God loved you enough to come into your world and show you the way past the wall. He came. He lived in our world. He spoke our language. He became intimately acquainted with the human condition. He loved. He laughed. He cried. He healed. He gave. Everything.

    And in so doing, He showed us the very heart of Father God.

        Jesus is the Explanation of Who Father God really is. And.

Not only is it His desire to lift away your "bread-crumb" burdens, lightening your life with His grace, and energizing you to live and breathe freely, (spiritually and emotionally), but He wants to take you on a journey to freedom --past the wall.

    And then --

        He wants to empower us to demolish our walls.

            For He loved us enough to become an ant.

The Father Has Chosen To Identify with You

"He brought me forth also into a broad place; He rescued me, because He delighted in me." Psalm 18:19

1. He watched a someone He had created to be a light-bearer (Lucifer) totally rebel against Him, and then turn the hearts of a company of the angels against Him, because they desired His position and glory. Those under His authority split the unity of Heaven, dividing it by their sinful rebellion and desire for control. *(Note: Anything that sets up its own control with a sense of independence from God's authority or delegated authority buys into the same deception).*

Is. 14:13-14
Rev. 12:3,7-9
Ezekiel 28:16-17

Make a list here of areas where you have experienced the pain of betrayal, and rejection.

_____

_____

2. He watched a Bride (Israel), for whom He had created and designed a Promised Land, turn away and give her affection to someone else.

Hosea 13:4-10
Matthew 23:37
Luke 13:34

List the areas of pain in your own life, where you have given love and love has not been returned.

_____

_____

3. He watched someone else raise His son on earth, without much more than limited visitation.

Luke 2:39-52
Hebrews 5:8-10
Philippians 2:5-11

List areas of pain in your life in regard to your parents or your children.

_____

_____

4. He watched His Son be betrayed and abandoned by His closest friends, setting Him up for a fall.

Mark 14:27
Mark 14:43-45

List areas of pain in your life when you have felt helpless to change a violent and lethal situation.

_____

_____

5. He watched strangers beat and murder His Son, when His Son had done nothing wrong.

Mark 15:15-37
Luke 20:9-18

List areas of pain in your life when you have lost something dear and precious to you through no fault of your own -those times when you have had a sense of being robbed, or stolen from -- violated.

_____

_____

Do you believe that Father God is able to bring resolution and healing to those areas of your life?

_____

_____

The Son Has Chosen to Identify With You

"For we do not have a high priest who cannot sympathize with our weaknesses, but One who has been tempted in all things as we are, yet without sin." Hebrews 4: 15

1. His mother conceived Him before she was married. Matthew 1:18 and 23

List areas of pain in your own life from rejection from peers and family here.

_____

_____

2. He was raised by a step-father. (Abba God Matthew 1:19-25
was His Father --not Joseph.) It is possible
He had two step-fathers. (Some scholars
believe that Alphaeus became Mary's husband
after Joseph's death.)

3. He was raised with half-brothers and Mark 3:31-35
half-sisters. (They shared only one parent-- Mary). Matthew 12:46-50

4. He was rejected by His earthly family. John 7:1-5

List areas of pain in your own life from blended family relationships, due to parental (or an authority figure's) marital unfaithfulness, abandonment, or divorce here.

_____

_____

5. He experienced physical limitations, and can Philippians 2:5-8
identify with handicapped individuals. (Limitless John 1:1-5
God took upon Himself the limits of flesh and blood. John 1:14-18
Imagine Almighty God dwelling inside a newborn
baby's body; completely uncoordinated; unable to
form words, unable to see clearly, unable to care for
Himself; waiting for weak, newborn legs to grow
and become able to support His body to stand and walk).

List areas of pain and frustration in your own life due to physical handicaps and weaknesses -- those areas you are willing to allow Jesus to touch with His own understanding and care.

_____

6. He was scoffed at by his home town,   Luke 4:16-30
who never received His ministry.

Jesus understands and has experienced the pain of rejection. List the areas pain due to rejection in your own life here.

_____

_____

7. He had no home of His own,   Matthew 8:20
and no dependable place to rest.   Luke 9:58

8. He didn't have enough money to pay   Matthew 17:24-27
His earthly taxes, and God the Father supplied

List areas of pain due to a lack of security here.

_____

_____

9. He was misunderstood   John 11:22-39

10. He was rejected   Isaiah 53:3
                                                                                       John 1:11
                                                                                       Luke 23:18

11. He was bruised   Luke 22:64
                                                                                       John 18:22

In what ways to you feel an identification with Jesus Christ (Father God in touchable form) after reading these Scriptures?

_____

_____

12. He was mocked and beaten   Luke 22:63-65

13. He was falsely accused, and then stripped of all following and position in the eyes of the earthly ruling powers.   Mark 14:57-58 / Matthew 27:11-14 / Luke 23:1-25

What injustices have you suffered that you are now realizing Father God understands?

_____

_____

14. He was kept up all night by his accusers.   Luke 22:45-53/63-71

15. He was spat upon and struck   Matthew 26:67

What violence have you experienced?

_____

_____

16. He was condemned to death as an innocent man.   Matthew 27:17-25

17. He was hated for no reason   John 15:24-25

18. He was betrayed by a close friend -- with a kiss --for money   Matthew 26:14-15 / Luke 22:47-48

19. He was scorned, jeered at and mocked   Luke 23:35-39

What rejection have you experienced?

_____

_____

20. His Father looked away when He needed Him most *(so that forever afterwards the Father could look through Jesus' eyes to see you – in your time of need).*

Matthew 27:45-46
Mark 15:33-34

What are your areas of need? Of what pain would you like to be free?

_____

_____

There is no pain of life experience with which Jesus Christ cannot identify… Abba Father came in the form of flesh, so that you would know just how very important it is to Him to give you freedom from your pain. He suffered violence, so that the results of that violence --the damage to your soul --could be washed away.

He wants to create a new heart within you.

Doesn't beginning all over again sound like a wonderful, and yet impossible illusion? But it is no illusion.

It is truth.

Abba Father, God, came in the form of skin and bone so show you the way through the wall. He is the only One who knows where you belong, and who you really are.

The first step in becoming free, is the willingness to admit that He *is* God, and that He is not the negative father who the enemy of your soul has painted Him to be through your life experiences.

He is who His Word says He is.

He always keeps His Word. He cannot lie.
        He has no ulterior motive. . He loves you.
                He will not violate you.
                        He wants to help you.

He wants to give you a Heavenly heritage to replace your earthly heritage.

He is your Father.

The second step is to release all of your pain into His hand. In the midst of your weeping, lift your hand off of the scratched knee, so your Papa can cleanse it and heal it. Yes, there will be tears, but they are tears that wash and cleanse, rather than deepen your grieving..

They are tears, which prepare your soul for the Presence of the Father.

It might be a little scary at first. After all, this is new territory.

You haven't been here before.

But didn't He promise never to let you fall?

Satan is Your Enemy
His Goal is to Bruise You

"The Spirit of the Lord is upon me to set the bruised at liberty." Luke 4: 18

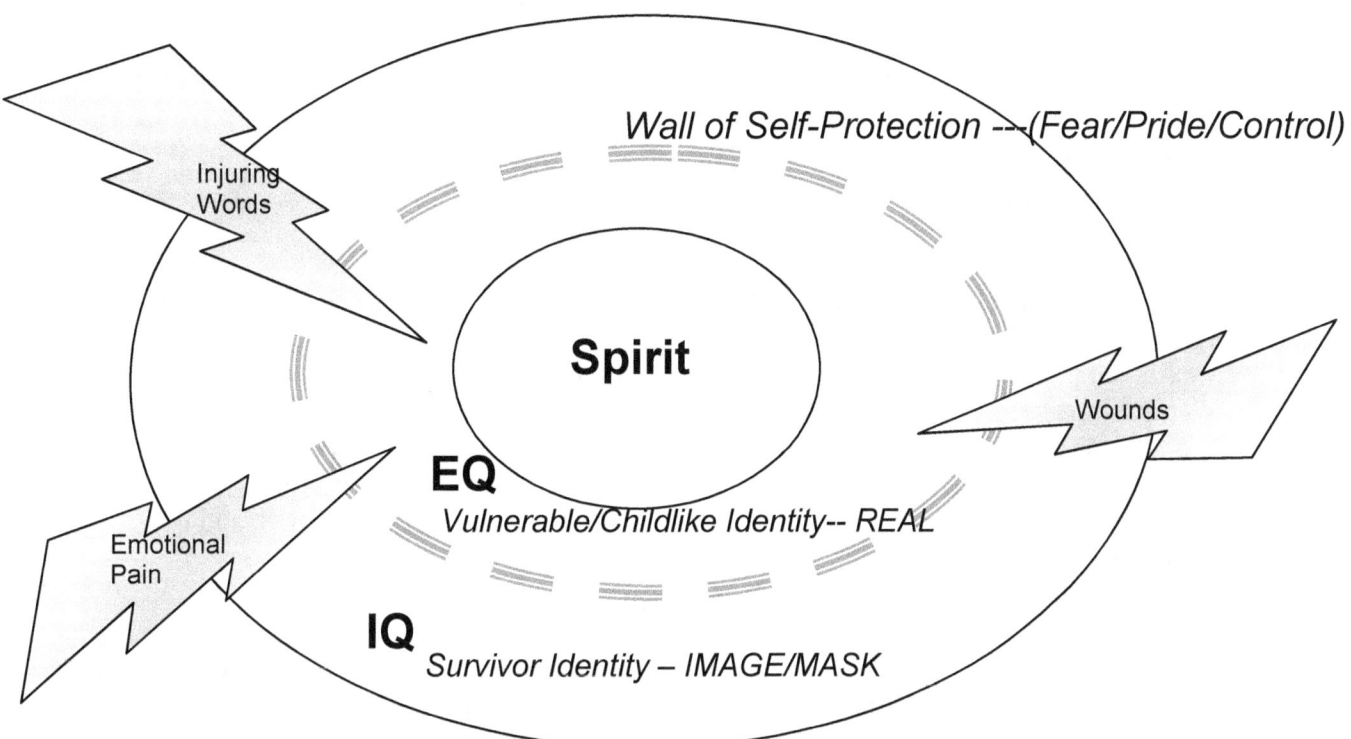

*A bruise is an area of pain within the soul.
It indicates an area of the human will which has experienced
crushing, or wounding; rendered weak or crippled,
unable to function in the manner which
the Creator, Abba Father God, intended.*

What promise does Isaiah 42:3 give regarding the ministry of Jesus to anything within the life that is bruised?

_____

_____

1. In the human body, a bruise occurs when the body receives a blow to muscles and tissue. At the point of impact, blood vessels swell, sometimes rupturing, filling the entire area with serum. The serum's purpose is to shield the injury from further damage, until healing is completed. In more serious cases, the area will even swell up, and complicate day-to-day actions and life processes. Every time the person tries to complete a task requiring the use of those bruised areas, the pain prevents full and free movement, reminding the person of the circumstances through which the bruise was received. In the same way, a bruise within the soul will hinder freedom in response to others, and will cause a person to shy away from having that area of their emotions touched by others. In hearts bruised from an early age, mechanisms for Self protection have hindered the person from becoming who they were designed to be by Father God, and they experience an inability to really relax and receive love. Identity and satisfaction begin to be found in achievements and accomplishments rather than in relationship.

What is Satan's agenda against us according to Genesis 3:15?
_____

3. The entire reason Satan exists is to bruise. It is his goal and purpose to stop anything closely resembling Father God from moving forward in growth or development. His ultimate plan is to make the process of walking through life impossible, or at the very least, impaired by crippling bruises, inflicted upon the human soul. Isaiah 28:28 gives us understanding the purpose of this bruising. *"Bread corn is bruised; because he will not ever be threshing it, nor break it with the wheel of his cart, nor bruise it with his horsemen."* Grain which has been bruised, cannot be threshed, or separated, and is therefore unusable.

Definition of Threshing: To separate the grain within from the chaff, or shell covering the kernel or seed. In Bible days, threshing was accomplished just below the top of a small hill. The "thresher" would use a large, flat basket, to toss the grain into the air, in a type of shaking process. While in the air, after it had hit the bottom of the basket, the inner grain was separated from its outer shell, or chaff. The wind would blow the chaff away, and the grain would fall to the ground, to be scooped up and put into storage.

The threshing process used in the New Testament illustrates the process of dividing the carnal, or fleshly and pride-based life, from the spiritual life.

What do these scriptures say about the ministry of threshing within the life of those who love Father God?

Matthew 3:11-12 _____

Luke 3:17-18 _____

Luke 22:31 _____

Matthew 13:24-30 _____

4. When grain is bruised, it cannot be threshed, or separated. In the same way, the purpose of Satan is to so crush the human heart (soul and spirit) that the person cannot distinguish between the voice of the soul and the voice of the spirit within them.

In what areas of your life do you have difficulty telling the difference between your soul and spirit?

_____

_____

What provision has Father God made to help us in distinguishing between these two areas? Read Hebrews 4:12.

_____

_____

Has the devil ever spoken doubt to you as to the inerrancy of the Scripture? Does this teaching shed new light on his reason for doing so? (If he can come against the source of healing, he can keep you in pain!!)

_____

5. The reason Jesus came was to provide liberty for those who are bruised. Often times, a bruised person fears the presence of the Lord, because they experience fear of the bruising being repeated, this time by Father God, and that fear overwhelms the heart. Matthew 12:20 promises us this:

"A bruised reed (it can't stand up on its own, needs a support, is weak) He will not break, and the smoking flax (almost ready to go out, has no flame), he will not quench, til he send forth judgment unto victory."

What does Hebrews 4:13-15 teach us about the ministry of Jesus? _____

_____

Scriptural definitions for bruising: to break, to shatter, smite through, to press, to be handled roughly, to be crushed, to be oppressed, to be discouraged, to struggle and oppress, to pulverize

Note: When a bruise is touched, it causes the entire area around it to hurt as well. After a bruise is inflicted upon a person's soul, all the enemy has to do is to remind them of the bruise in some way, and the entire area hurts all over again.

The Bruised Soul

*"The Spirit of the Lord is upon me, because he hath anointed me to preach the gospel to the poor; he hath sent me to heal the brokenhearted, to preach deliverance to the captives, and recovering of sight to the blind, **to set at liberty them that are bruised.**"* Luke 4: 18

The Human Soul (mind, will, & emotions)

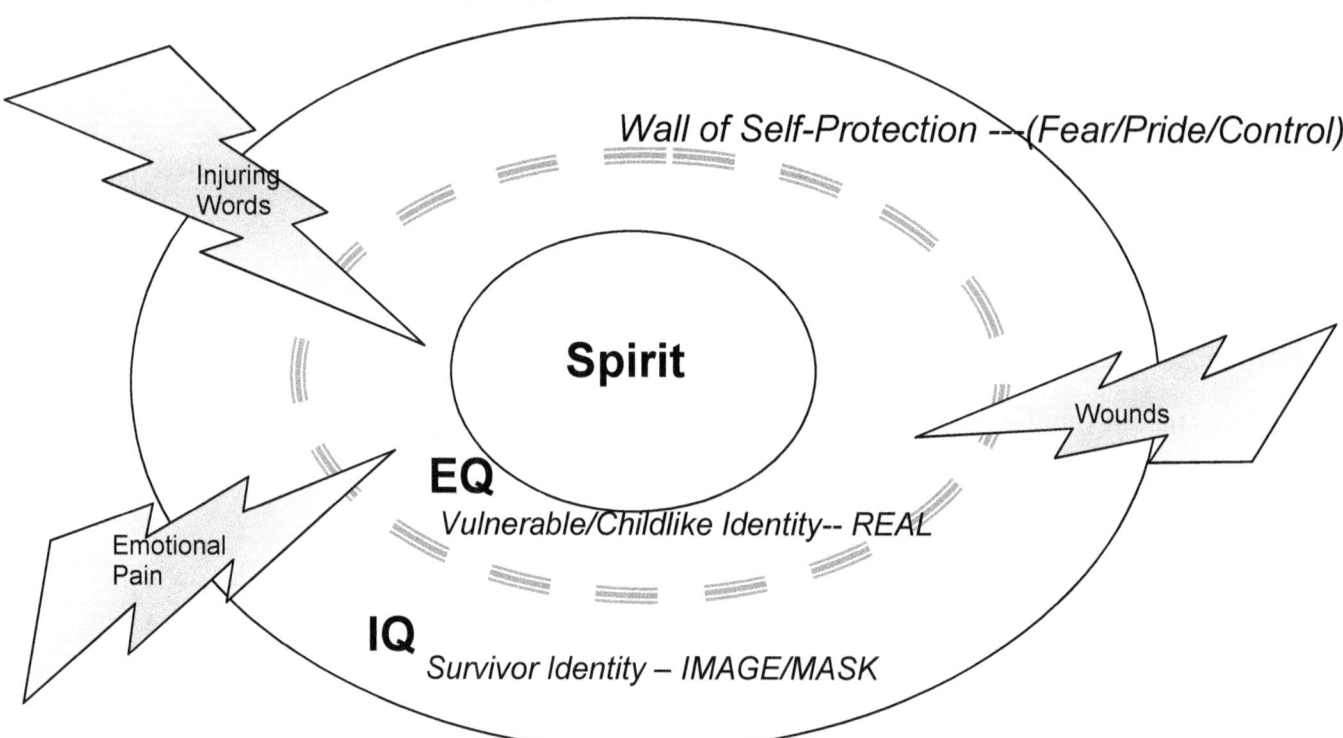

Following the willful sin of Adam in the Garden of Eden, the Father spoke the following words to the serpent:

"And I will put enmity between thee and the woman,. and between thy seed (sin and death) and her seed (Jesus Christ): it shall bruise (crush) thy head; and thou shalt bruise his heel." Genesis 3: 15

This scripture indicates that it is Satan's purpose to bruise. He knows how to impede a person's walk with a bruise. He knows how to cripple a person with bruising. It is his intention to cause every person on the planet to become defensive in their lives and relationships, protecting those bruises inflicted by his nature.

When Jesus paid the price: for sin on the Cross, as Perfect God and Perfect Man, he took the effect of our bruises upon Himself.

"Yet it pleased the Lord to bruise Him; he hath put Him to grief." Isaiah 28:28

"But He was wounded for our <u>transgressions, he was bruised for our iniquities:</u> the chastisement of our peace was upon Him, and with His stripes, we are healed." Isaiah 53:5

So then, what is a bruise?

Description: The response and condition of the human <u>heart,</u> which has been exposed to the nature of the enemy, the devil. In Old Testament scripture, this is also referred to as a "broken spirit."

Purpose of Bruises: To destroy the peace of God within the soul; to prevent a person from being able to receive or to sense peace; to slow the advancement and growth of the believer in peace; to destroy within the heart and conscience, the ability to distinguish between soul and spirit.

> To open the door to bondages.
>
> To cause a person to live without positive emotion.
>
> To torment with emotional memories.
>
> To destroy God given Personhood and identity.

Consider what we have studied so far. Many times, when a bruise is surfacing in the soul, we experience memories, have dreams, or find ourselves thinking of places of past pain. This is usually the work of the Holy Spirit, who is showing us the source of the bruises we have experienced in our lives. What bruises have come to mind in our study so far? Write them here.

The Infliction of Bruises, and How They Occur in the Life

words
being the object of another's anger
physical abuse
punishment instead of discipline (children)
absence or abuse of corporal discipline (children)
sexual abuse
molestation
masturbation
rejection
betrayal
severed relationships
divorce and marital separation
conditional relationships
isolation
death of someone close
self hatred
self rejection
loneliness
fantasies
competition
criticism
perfectionist expectations
being put-down
lack of acceptance
false teachings
deception
generational weaknesses
alcoholism – any of the "isms"
failures
disobedience
mental illness
physical deformities
failure to meet expectations --of others
failure to meet expectations --of self
authority's expectations not communicated

We were each born in trespasses and sins.

> *"Wherefore, as by one man sin entered into the world, and death by sin; and so death passed upon all men, for that all have sinned." Romans 5:12*

Because of Adam's choice to sin in Eden, reign and dominion of the human soul, and the planet were given, because of his trickery, to Satan.

And sin grows with each generation, until it is broken by the Blood of the Lamb.

> *"The Lord is longsuffering and of great mercy, forgiving iniquity and transgression, and by no means clearing the guilty, visiting the iniquity of the fathers upon the children unto the third and fourth generation." Numbers 14:18 --(Deuteronomy 5:9, Exodus 20:5, and 34:7)*

Every person born on the planet, is born with the influences of Rejection. In its final stages, Rejection becomes Rebellion --an individual's personal and expressed rejection of Father God. In addition, because man is created in the image of Father God, just that presence within a life brings a person to the practice of self-rejection.

The nature of our enemy, Satan, the destroyer, is seen in the Wall and spirit of Pride. (Isaiah 14:12-15) Pride speaks a false identity to a person. It projects perfection, when there is no perfection. It exalts without humility. It puffs up without the knowledge of God. It finds its strength in the world's wisdom, without the wisdom of God. It seeks to mix earthly and spiritual kingdoms, with no confrontation of self. This is Satan's personality, and it calls for and welcomes demonic involvement within a person's life.

Moreover, because Satan works in violent hatred, against anything reminding him of his Creator, and Judge, he and his henchmen strive religiously to destroy anything with any hint of the image of Father God.

They hate you. They don't need you to give them a reason.

It is enough for them that you are breathing air provided by Your Creator. Even before you became a follower of Jesus Christ, it was more than enough for them that you carried the potential to become eternally alive. You simply look like Him – because you are three parts – as He is…..

They reject you. They work within the world and its systems to reject you.

They deceive you with Pride, knowing that any Pride within your own heart will rule your life through Rejection. It continually speaks of your failure to achieve perfection. They remind you of your sins and weaknesses, until Hope is quenched and the flow of the Spirit's Joy is stilled.

"You will never attain," they say. "This is just the way it is."

And yet,

       the strategy they use is to convince you

              that this is your own doing
              that you will always know this pain
              that this is just the way life is

has no weight or value when placed in comparison with the Light and Love of Father God.

    Jesus said,

"The devil… was a murderer from the beginning, and did not abide in truth because there is no truth in him. When he speaks a lie, he speaks his own,

    For he is a liar, and the father of lies."   (John 8:44-45)

    "I am the Truth."   (John 14:6)

    "You shall know the Truth, and the Truth shall set you free." (John 8:32)

Satan is Your Enemy
His Goal is the Wound You

"The soul of the wounded cries out" Job 24: 12

**To wound: (from Hebrew and Greek root word definitions)
to beat, to cause sores, to bruise, to hurt,
to cause sorrow, to leave with an appetite for more,
to break into pieces.**

1. Physical wounds bleed, and Father God hears the cry of the wounded person, from the person's blood.	Genesis 4: 10 (Hebrews 4:10)
2. The heart mourns, grieving losses.	Jeremiah 48:31

What wounds "speak" to you, within your own heart, reminding you of past incidences, keeping you from knowing the joy in life the Father has for you?

_____

3. Words cause wounds, and bruises. (Hebrew definition: leaving an appetite for more)	Proverbs 18:8 Proverbs 26:22
4. Wounds stink when they are caused by foolish behavior. Such wounds are corrupt in God's sight.	Psalm 38:5

Do you seem to gravitate towards negative images regarding your life, remembering words and expectations from your past, which have wounded you?

_____

What wounding words have you allowed yourself to identify with?

_____

Because words of this kind "desire more," a wounded human soul will remember hurtful words more easily than kind or gracious words. These types of words will take on more depth and identification within the person's heart and life. This is the devil's way of continuing the pain, and the bondage cycles of Rejection. Read Psalm 107:20, and Matthew 8:5-10. What do these scriptures teach about the words Father God speaks over your life?

_____

_____

Count-Down

Down through the years, He had looked for those who would incline their hearts toward Him. He had searched the hearts of man and could see what they consisted of. Here and there, through time since Eden, He had found those who wanted His fellowship. There had been those who searched for Him; for His solution and blessing.

First there had been Seth, and then Enoch. There had been good fellowship with Enoch. Enoch was a good friend.

Then there had been Noah --and Abraham.

Abraham had been a joy. He had been so eager for blessing, he had left everything behind, just to find the Promised Land of Canaan. So, it had been to Abraham, He had given Faith. Nothing could stand between Abraham and the Promise. It had been to Abraham that He had first shared the seeds of the Plan.

Then there had been Joseph. Joseph had had to pay dearly for His time spent with the Father as a child. Nevertheless, he had learned the heart of Abba Father. During the days he had been in prison, as a slave in Egypt, they had shared such sweet times together. It was during those days that Joseph had learned what it meant to forgive. It had been tremendous joy to the Father's heart to watch Joseph as he had lived out those private lessons of the heart.

He had forgiven so much.

Then there had been Moses. Moses had been another living illustration of Father God. This time, it was His desire to free His people from slavery. It had been a two-fold lesson. Not only did the Father want His people free from Pharaoh's cruelty, He also wanted them free within --from Satan's bruises and bondages. It had been physical illustration of the Plan.

Seeing by example was the only way, man could understand.

****

Contemplative, Jesus stood on the road in Galilee, remembering and thinking. He smiled.

The past forty days had been the culmination of three years. Walking and living out before those who had followed Him the meaning and example of carrying the Life of God inside human skin and bones. During that time, He had given them every morsel of truth they could absorb. They had absorbed much.

Also during that time, Satan had played his hand of evil and trickery.

The rebellion was still alive.

The Cross had been a bitter cup. He had known it would be before Moses, before Eden, before Creation.

It was all part of the Plan.

Jesus looked up the road in anticipation. They were meeting Him here. Today was the day!!

There were eleven left.

One had made the same choice Adam had made in Eden. He had chosen Self, and Satan had filled His heart. Jesus pitched a small stone into the field as He thought of Judas.

He had seen that inclination *before* Creation as well.

Another one had walked away. One of three whom He had poured His very Life into. One from the three; the inner circle. Peter had denied even *knowing* Him. Three times.

Jesus smiled when He thought of Peter.

The Comforter would heal those weaknesses and fears. Oh, there were great days ahead for Simon!!

There were great days ahead for all of them! Even for Thomas.

Mary Magdalene was the first one to arrive at the launch site. She fell at His feet, much like another woman so long ago in Eden. She also was weeping; but today's tears were tears of joy and of worship.

"Master!" she greeted Him. This was the gentle voice of a delicate and feminine expression, redeemed from the very mouth of Hell. This woman had received a re-birth of spirit. She knew the Source of her life.

Peter ran to meet the Expression of the Father. He grabbed Jesus in one of those bear hugs, which only men who have worked outside, in the heat of day, and have developed camaraderie can understand.

This was a restored life.

A life on a journey of healing.

He was forgiven and he knew it, deep inside. The fear of man's disapproval was losing its hold on Peter. He was learning to hold on to the Father with his whole heart.

There were so many others.

They knew He was going today. He had told them about the preparations.
                                                              There were tears and good-byes.

He spoke to them tenderly. He lifted up their heads. He smiled through His sadness. But it was a sadness mingled with anticipation. He spoke.

"We can still be together, you know. But it will be easier now --for you."

And then --

He told them of the Gift He was sending: Of the Comforter, the Teacher, the Enabler, the Power. He told them of the Holy Spirit.

He told them that no longer would the battle against the sinful elements of the soul be so difficult.

He told them that their re-born spirits within had been filled with the Spirit of God, and not too many days away He would send Empowerment to live life on earth as He had lived. A Mighty Wind. The Spirit of God would not only be *upon* them, it would be *within* them as well.

Not only would they be able to conquer the sinful soul, but they would lead others out of darkness as well!

The adversary's design was halted now -- from two directions!

It would only be 10 days or so --He would send the Spirit on the feast day so they would really have something to celebrate!! The Feast Day was Pentecost --a time when they traditionally celebrated Liberty anyway! He wanted them to understand, and remember --

        Liberty is what the Spirit of God is all about.

                    "I'll be with you always. Even to the end of the world."

And then, with His eyes on the reunion with the Father, He was lifted up. They looked up and watched, until He was out of sight. Then they hurried to Jerusalem; to pray; to wait; to feast on all He had given them. Their hearts were full of joy.

They could feel it deep within -- things were only to get better.

        A glorious Empowering was on its way.

****

The ruling forces of darkness began to shudder when they saw the Resurrection. They trembled in fear when the Father reclaimed the Path into Paradise. They unwillingly and vacillatingly fell on their faces, momentarily weak when Christ declared His Lordship.

But if they had had any idea what was coming through the lives of spiritually re-born believers –

If they had had any concept of the power of God which would be released against them through obedient members of the Bride of Christ --

    They never would have crucified Him.

Christ in me.
    Christ in you.
        The Incarnation – over and over again.

The Hope of Glory;
    manifesting the mysteries of God in the heavenly realm;
        showing what His power really is.

We were the Plan.

    YOU were the Plan.

> Please listen to the fourth CD, utilizing your notebook, for
> Session Four
>
> "The Generational Fruits of Fathering"
> before you move ahead

Notes:

The Companion

When I was a little girl, my parents traveled a great deal. Mom and Dad served as itinerant missionaries with a well-known ministry. We spent many nights in church services in varied churches both in the United States and overseas. Dad shared the Gospel, and Mom would minister from the piano.

One of my childhood memories occurred when I was around nine years old. Our family had completed our tenure of ministry in Sydney, Australia. We were on the TWA jet, coming back to the United States. "We're going home," my mother said. I was really looking forward to seeing all the things my parents had described to me. I remember wanting to visit my grandparents. Most of all, I wanted to taste an American hamburger!!

When we disembarked the plane, two smiling faces greeted us at the gate. There were hugs, greetings, and "how was your trip's?" all around. I remember thinking how nice it was to be with people who loved us. It felt good.

Then, since I was the youngest in the crowd, the couple asked me where I thought we should go to eat. I didn't have the foggiest notion. This was an entirely new country to me. One thing I do remember. I asked for a hamburger. They proceeded to introduce me to MacDonald's.

The experience became an imprinting moment. I still love "quarter pounders with cheese!" I thought it must be the closest thing to Heaven! But then, I was nine!!

I can remember many similar experiences whenever we traveled. Someone was always there to help us, to show us the way, to lead us in caravan to the church, to explain, to prepare, to warn, to interpret. Sometimes they were close friends of my parents, and sometimes they were strangers.

Specifically, I remember when we traveled in the nation of Belgium. Everyone was fluent in French except me. An ancient (or so she seemed to me!), "grandmother," took time to explain her country to me. "Why do they do that?' "How do you say _____?" "What is that statue?" --We also played a fun game of hide and seek together on a rainy afternoon. She also taught me to speak understandable French.

It was like having my own personal tour guide.

I also remember times when we traveled that I was afraid: new experiences, new places, new faces, new pillows and bedrooms. Nevertheless, there was always someone to help ease my difficulty in the journey. When Dad and Mom were unable to be with me, someone else was always there.

I was never alone.

In a consistent and identical manner, the Holy Spirit ministers to us as believers. He is the Presence of Father God. He is everywhere. We are never alone. He has come to comfort, to explain, to teach, to guide, to warn, to protect, and to nurture.

His mission is to help us to see Jesus, and thereby understand Father God. He is the one who speaks comfort and encouragement to our souls. He is the One who says, "This is the way. Walk here."

Moreover, when the enemy of our heart whispers his dark threatenings, it is the Holy Spirit, the very Presence of Father God, Who reminds us of his doom, and puts Hope within our grasp.

For --

> Since Jesus is the Explanation of the Nature of Father God,
>
> > It is the Holy Spirit, the Enabler, who does the explaining.

The Ministry of the Holy Spirit

"The Spirit also helps us in our weaknesses." Romans 8:26

As you go through the following explanations of the personality and scriptural explanations of the Holy Spirit, make a note on the lines provided of any fresh understanding and acceptance of His ministry, that you are realizing now is available for your life.

The Holy Spirit, the Presence of Father God, is known by the following names in Scripture:

a. Eternal Spirit
(Grk. = "aionios" without beginning or ending, and has always been.)

Christ offered Himself through the Eternal Spirit without Blemish to God. He has always existed with God the Father

Hebrews 9:14

b. Free Spirit
(Heb. ="nadiyb", willing, inclined to be generous)

"Uphold me by Thy free Spirit." (He is willing and inclined to be generous to help those seeking to obey the Father.)

Psalm 51:12

_____

_____

c. Spirit of Knowledge and The Fear of the Lord
(Heb. = "da-ath", know-ledge, perception, skill, discernment, understanding, wisdom --& "yirah", exceeding respect and reverence; Realization of awe.)

This is the Spirit of the Lord which manifested in Jesus Christ, the "Branch, from the Root of Jesse." (The Spirit of the Lord knows our own heart when we do not, and will help us to walk in the fear of the Lord.)

Isaiah 11:2

d. Spirit of Counsel and Might
(Heb. = "etsah", counsel, advice, and purpose --& "buwrah", might, valor, bravery, power, force, mastery")

This is the Spirit of the Lord which manifested in Jesus Christ, the "Branch from the Root of Jesse." (The Spirit of the Lord will help us by empowering us to be obedient. He will help us to battle our carnal flesh.)

Isaiah 11:2

_____

_____

e. Spirit of Grace and Supplications (Heb. = "chen", favor, acceptance, --& "tachanuwn," an appeal, or entreaty for favor (forgiveness) to man as well as to God.	Opens the eyes of man to see and understand the fruit of his actions, and enables the heart to seek God's favor. (He will enable us to ask for forgiveness).	Zechariah 12:10
f. Spirit of Grace (Grk. = "charis") that which gives joy, pleasure, delight, and loveliness. Good-will, the merciful kindness of God – that which draws souls to Christ, and then keeps and strengthens them in Christian growth)	The Spirit which causes obedience, and an awareness of the gift of the Life of God through Jesus Christ. (He will help us to see how great the love and mercy of the Father are toward us. He will help us to understand and sense the great love and Presence of God.)	Hebrews 10:29
g. Good Spirit (Heb. = "towb", good, precious, valuable in estimation, ethical, appropriate, pleasant)	The Lord gave His Spirit to instruct (Heb. = "sakal" understand, be circumspect to prosper and have success) the children of Israel. (The Spirit will help us to walk in an ethical manner, honest with both God and man).	Nehemiah 9:20

h. Spirit of Prophecy (Grk. = "propheteia," a divinely inspired declaration of the purposes of God. Reproves, admonishes, comforts and reveals.)	The testimony of Jesus is the Spirit of Prophecy. (The Holy Spirit will enable us to speak of Jesus and Him crucified He enables those five-fold offices within the church government to move according to His plan. The Spirit enables the ministry of the prophetic within the church as well.)	Revelation 19: 10
i. Spirit of Life (Grk. = "zoe", every living soul, an active and full life, which is consecrated and set apart to God, operating ethically and morally.)	Gives life and liberty. (The Holy Spirit will help us to stay free from bondage and fear, living according to the law of the Spirit of life).	Romans 8:2 (Revelation 11: 11)
j. Spirit of Truth (Grk. = "aletheia" what is true in any matter, free from affection, pretence, simulation, falsehood, or deceit)	The Helper. He will guide us into all truth, because He speaks what the Father says. Those who do not listen to sound doctrine have the spirit of error. (The Holy Spirit will help us to be teachable and walk in the Truth of the Word.)	John 16:13 John 15:26 John 14:17 I John 4:6

k. Spirit of Glory (Grk. = "doxa", splendor, brightness, magnificence, dignity, kingly majesty, a most exalted state, absolute perfection)	The Spirit of Glory rests upon us as believers. When we are reviled --rejoice! (The Holy Spirit will draw us from glory to glory, as we are changed into the image and likeness of Jesus Christ).	I Peter 4:14 (ll Corinthians 3: 17-18)
1. Spirit of Promise (Grk. = "epaggelia", announcement, or promise of blessing)	The Spirit who speaks the remembrance of the Father's character and nature toward those who believe. (He has sealed us into the hand of the Father, as being saved from destruction.)	Ephesians 1:13
m. Spirit of Revelation (Grk. = "apokalupsis" reveal, laying something bare, to make naked, to disclose truth and instruction, to cause to manifest or appear.)	The Spirit Who knows all things, and sees within the heart of man - what needy areas there exist within us. (He will disclose the nature of the Father to us in our point of need.)	Ephesians 1: 17 (I Corinthians 2: 10) (Ephesians 3:5)

n. Spirit of Wisdom (Grk. = "sophia" the wisdom of God, Supreme Intelligence, as seen in forming the order of creation and the counsels of Scripture)	He knows the Ways and Counsels of the Father, and discloses them to those with a heart seeking to know and understand God's purposes and ways. (He will disclose to us the wisdom of God, enlightening the heart of man to know the Father's plan.)	Ephesians 1:17-18 (I Kings 4:29) (Job 36:5) (James 3:14-18)
o. Spirit of Wisdom (Heb. = "chokmah" Skill in warfare, Wise administration Prudence and ethical practices)	The Spirit of the Lord gives wisdom in warring against the enemy forces, and imparts the ability to rule and design with skill. (He will help us to accomplish everything the Father gives us to do).	Exodus 28:3 Deuteronomy 34:9
p. Spirit of Faith (Grk. = "pistis" the conviction and assurance that something is true, has fidelity, and can be trusted as reliable.)	He imparts faith. (Without His enablement, we cannot believe God. He helps us to believe.)	II Corinthians 4: 13 (Galatians 3:5 and 14) (I Corinthians 12:9)

q. Spirit of Meekness (Grk. = "praotes" gentleness, mildness)	The expressed nature of Christ through believers. (He will show that nature in us as we choose to obey His Word).	1 Corinthians 4:21 (Galatians 5:23) (Galatians 6:1) (Ephesians 4:2) (Colossians 3: 12) (1 Timothy 6: 11) (Titus 3:2)
r. Spirit of Holiness (Grk. = "hagiosune" Majesty, holiness, moral purity)	That Spirit which declares Jesus to be the resurrected Son of God, and to which state we are called as believers. (He will establish us as holy, without blame before God, as we seek His power to cleanse us from all remnants of the kingdom of darkness).	Romans 1:4 II Corinthians 7: 1 I Thessalonians 3:13

New Horizons!! Lessons for Liberty

Part Two –

"Designed and Destined"

The Make-Up of Man

*"And God created man in His own image, in the likeness of God
He created them, male and female He created them." Genesis 1:27*

God created Adam as a three-part being

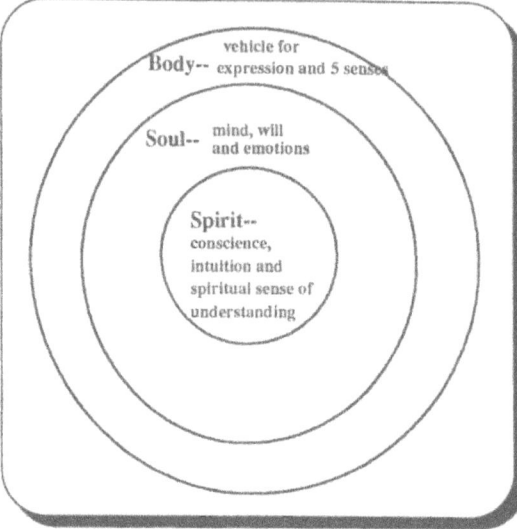

1. BODY -That part of man, which is physically seen, and has tangible feeling. It's nature is understood by the abilities to touch, see, hear, smell, and taste. It is the vehicle through which the desires and choices of the soul and spirit are expressed and carried out. It is the vessel. (Luke 12:22)

2. SOUL -That unseen part of man, which is the seat of his personality and desires. It's nature can be seen in man's ability to distinguish between pain and pleasure, whether physical or responsive (the emotions), his ability to choose and distinguish between right and wrong,-- also choices made in regard to those perceptions (the will), and his ability to think in reasonable patterns for development of communication and understanding (the mind). (Matthew 22:37) Prior to regeneration, the soul is under the bondage and dominion of Satan. It's natural nature is to be consumed with itself, and its own gratification. The soul must be made new and transformed into the likeness of Jesus following the re-birth of the spirit of man. (II Corinthians 3:18) It is the place of battle in the believer. **The soul is the unseen part of our being that is aware and drawn to the physical realm by appetites.**

3. SPIRIT -That unseen part of man, which comprises his ability to communicate from the depths of his being with His Creator. It comprises his conscience, his inner spiritual sense, and his intuition. (John 3:1-20) Without regeneration by the Spirit of God, it is dead and is full of the desire to sin. [Adam was made a living soul, and willfully gave the life of his spirit over to the enemy. Jesus Christ was made a quickening (life-giving, resurrecting) Spirit, so that all who call upon Him are able to be delivered; from darkness (the desire to sin) into light (the desire to please the Father). That choice to follow Christ and receive His gift of Life, brings a regeneration of the spirit in the inner man.] Regeneration is the only hope man has to regain the eternal life and freedom which Adam lost through his willful sin. (1 Corinthians 15:44-45/Romans 6:5-11/John 3: 16/Romans 5:8-19 and 6:6) **The spirit is the unseen part of our being that is aware and drawn to the eternal realm through relationship with Jesus Christ and Abba Father.**

Condemnation

"You failed again."

The whispered accusation lingered in the man's mind, like a suspended mist. For a few moments the human face contorted with the repeated realization of what he had done.

"The Holy Spirit told you not to do it, and you did it anyway. You'll never be strong. You'll never make a difference."

The man had stopped. He was listening.

The whispers gained momentum.

"You are such a weakling. You've never made a strong stand. What do you think people would think about you, if they really knew your weaknesses?"

The man stopped writing and shut his eyes.

"There's no forgiveness left, you know. How many times have you asked Him to cover this same sin? It's too late now. There's no hope for you."

Suddenly aware, the apostle Paul thrust down his quill. He rose to his feet and began to pace the room, agitated.

And the whisperer continued. He had been assigned to stop this letter. The church in Rome must not receive encouragement; Not now; Not when the persecution was just mounting, and beginning to succeed. His orders had come from the deepest of the darkness.

He whispered again. He had this human distracted.

"How can you call yourself an apostle? You're just full of yourself. It's pride; Nothing more."

The man of God looked through the shutters and out the window. There were children playing in the street. He remembered the days of his youth.

Before.

He had gone to synagogue school with the other boys. He had loved the discussions and the learning processes. He had been fascinated with Gamaliel's way of explaining the law. His teacher had made it easy to listen. He had made it fun.

Then, he had been groomed to be a Pharisee. It was his destiny, they said. He had been born to that position.
It ran in the family.

He smiled at the idea now; A Pharisee.

Was this his own idea?

****

The Enabler was also in the room. He was communicating with Abba Father, setting boundaries for the enemy in this attack. He was watching, and waiting to be asked for help. Satan's pawns could go no further than they were allowed to.

Paul would need strength for the times ahead of him. This present wrestling was building his spiritual muscles for days to come.

****

Abba Father was watching as well; also remembering those early days….

Paul, or rather Saul, as he had been called then, had always inclined his heart and mind --and his will-- towards the Father. Strong headed – also instilled at birth -- Once the boy was shown that a path was right and profitable, it was very hard to stop him --or even to change his mind!!

He was determined to obey God.

It had been this part of his nature, which the Father had chosen for His purposes. There had been a time when Saul had murdered those faithful believers involved in the newly birthed, infant Church --he had been a real tool of Satan against Her.

He had believed the path was right. He was honest, full of zeal, and trying with all of his heart to please the Father.

But how can you please Someone you don't know? How can you develop relationship with Someone you only have a head-knowledge of?

In addition, he had been so bound by traditions and empty formalism; following a *copy* of Abba's plan without its power. His supposed power had been his own. – and sometimes fueled by something worse.

All it had taken was an Encounter.

****

Paul continued to stand by the window, and his re-born spirit began to stir within. Suddenly, the image of a brilliant and sustained lightning flashed into the recesses of his memory.

He had fallen off his donkey. Then there had been that voice; that lustrous and amazing voice.

"Saul! Saul! Why are you persecuting Me?"

Persecuting? What was this vision? He hadn't been *persecuting* anyone! He was following the orders of the religious rulers. He was under authority. He knew what to do!!

But the Voice. The fear of the Lord within his heart was awakened. He had stuttered, and covered his eyes.

"Who are You, Lord?"

The Voice, ever so full of awesome power, yet ruled by mercy, replied. "I am Jesus, who you are persecuting."

Suddenly, in a split second of time, Saul could see his Choice. He had been walking in the right direction, but with the wrong understanding!! The Law of the Father became real to His heart -- Almost tangible!!

"Oh, Almighty God! I am a man of unclean heart!" he cried. "I see! I see it now!"

"I will choose the Light!! I choose to follow Your Ways --not just Your doings! I want to know you."

In the series of events following, when Saul had come back into physical reality, he had found himself physically blind. But it didn't matter. He wasn't even hungry. Oh, his spirit could now see!! He understood. For three days, he feasted upon the goodness of Father God.

In those days of physical blindness, the young Saul began to realize just to what depth his soul had been blind until now. The Scriptures he had studied so well began to come alive in his understanding. The God he had learned about, debated about, and presented was different entirely from anyone he had thought he understood. This was a loving God, a good God, and patient God, who loved His creation, and desired relationship. God was not just a far removed, Demander of perfection, Giver of the Law. No, the Light of God had exposed the deception in his soul.

An explosion of Liberty within his soul had kindled a fire which he would never allow to die. His life was changed.

He would never be the same again.

Moreover, neither would the Church. He knew his life had a mission.

His mind came back to the present.

No. He had not made it up! !

****

The whispering, accusing being sat in the corner. He could not read Paul's thoughts, but he knew something was happening on the other side of the room.

At least the man wasn't writing.

He decided to say one more thing -- Just one more. He could really make this visit count if he used the right strategies.

****

"Why don't you give up? It's not worth the trouble."

"You could be doing something so much bigger than this."

The man of God spoke. "Father, please help me in my weakness."

That was **all** it took.

Immediately, angels stood around the righteous man who was wrestling desperately in the midst of his heart and soul, with swords drawn to defend him. The Spirit of God ceased waiting and began to blow gently upon him, inspiring, giving Life, restoring Liberty and Joy. Peace began to rule in the room.

And the former Pharisee, a citizen of two nations, high-born,
        Redeemed, transformed, filled and infused with the Spirit of God,

 took action.

"Be Gone!! Get out in the name of Jesus Christ, the Lord I serve!"

Shadows and heaviness began to lift from the room.

Paul's thought processes began to take on a new order. He crumpled the papyrus he had begun in his own strength several hours previous, and with new fervor and understanding, began to write.

> *"For we know the Law is spiritual; but I am made of flesh and blood, and have been sold into bondage to sin: Because I don't understand the things I do; I want to do one thing, but find myself doing the very thing I hate. But I see a different law in the members of my body, waging war against the law of my mind, and making me a prisoner of the law of sin which is in my members. On one hand I am serving the law of God with my mind, but on the other, with my flesh I am serving the law of sin. But there is now no condemnation to those who are in Christ Jesus. For the law of the Spirit of Life in Christ Jesus has set me free from the law of sin and death. What the law could not do, weak as it was through the flesh, God did; sending His own Son in the likeness of sinful flesh, and as an offering for sin, He condemned sin in the flesh."*

The demon fled. This had become a pointless exercise.

> Please listen to the fifth CD, utilizing your notebook, for
> Session Five
>
> "Addressing the Wall of Pride"
> before you move ahead

Notes:

The Spirit of Man

*Jesus answered and said to unto him, "Truly I say to you,
unless a man is born again he cannot see the Spirit of God."* John 3:3

Problem: The unregenerate (fallen) spirit of man is dead in trespasses and sins, because of the willful choice made in Eden. (see Genesis 2:1-3:24, John 3:5-7)

Solution: The spirit must be re-born into the spiritual realm. (John 3: 1-21)

At the point of salvation, an explosion of the Light and Liberty of the Spirit of God recharges the spirit with the power of God, making it spiritually alive, as Adam was before he chose to disobey. (Ephesians 2:1-6)

The overflow of this explosive work touches the soul, and the need for change is realized. (Colossians 2:13-14)

Principle: In order to receive Life, the root operating system of man must be changed from death to life, from darkness to light.

An Overview of the Unregenerate Human Spirit

1. The Human Spirit is formed by Father God within man, and man has no power over its destiny once the body dies.

   Zechariah 12:1
   Ecclesiastes 8:8

2. The spirit is dead, subject to the ruler of Sin and the Flesh. No cutting away of the selfish covering (walls) of the soul has occurred.

   Ephesians 2: 1
   Colossians 2: 13

3. The soul is alive, but the human spirit must be quickened, or made alive by the Spirit of Jesus Christ, the last Adam.

   I Corinthians 15:45

Has your spirit been quickened (made alive) by the Spirit of God?

_____

4. The natural, or sin-ruled, man cannot understand spiritual principles. They appear foolish to him. He is blinded by the god of this world (the devil) (How can he understand spiritual things when his spirit has not yet been made alive?)

   I Corinthians 2: 14
   II Corinthians 3: 12-18
   II Corinthians 4:3-4

What spiritual truths would you like to understand and comprehend to a greater degree?

_____

_____

5. When the Spirit of God does not dwell in a person, they can have no part of the provisions Christ has made for wholeness.

   Romans 8:9

6. No one can live a happy and fulfilled, holding an non-regenerated, wounded human spirit.

   Proverbs 18:14

Do you know where your spirit (the real you, the inner person) will spend eternity? Where? (If you are not sure where you will spend eternity, this indicates that you need to receive Jesus Christ as your Lord and Savior. Just ask Him, right now, to come into your life, forgive you sins, and help you to live you life for Him from this point onward. Then, find a good church where you can be fed as a Christian, and grow in His Word and Way.)

Qualities of the Regenerated Human Spirit

1. The inbreathing (inspiration) of the life of Almighty   Proverbs 17:27
   God (Father God) gives man understanding. The beginning   Job 32:8
   of this ministry in the human spirit is the mark of the   Psalm 111:10
   fear of the Lord. (The fear of the Lord is the awareness of   Proverbs 1:7
   the awesomeness and vastness of Father God's presence).   Proverbs 9: 10

What evidences of new birth, via the fear of the Lord do you see in your own life? (Note-- The Fear of the Lord is not an afraid of fear, but an awareness of who Father God is and His capabilities.)

_____

_____

2. We cannot understand or perceive the things,   John 3:5-7
   which comprise the Kingdom of God without being   I Peter 1:23
   born again of the Spirit of God. This new birth is
   the beginning of eternal life.

What evidences of new birth, via the understanding of spiritual things, do you see in your own life?

_____

_____

3. Jesus Christ will strengthen us with His might in   Ephesians 3:16-19
   the inner man (the spirit and soul). He will help us
   to comprehend the love of Christ, which passes
   knowledge, and be filled with the fullness of God.

In what areas do you need to be strengthened with the mighty of Jesus Christ to understand His love for you?

_____

_____

    4. When we speak by the Spirit of God, we cannot curse God, use His name in vain, or move outside of the leadership of Father God. The Spirit of God will always call Jesus, "Lord." Without the Spirit of God working in our lives, we do not recognize that Jesus Christ is actually Father God in the form of human skin and bone.   I Corinthians 12:3

Without the realization that Jesus Christ is actually Father God, come in human form, we do not have the key to the spiritual power; nor can we unlock chains of bondage in our lives. The most subtle tool of Satan and his forces is to undermine trust and belief in Christ's Deity.

What is the importance of that truth in your own life? In what way do you need to apply it to your own understanding?

_____

    5. When the human spirit is full of the Spirit of the Lord (born again), it acts as the searchlight of the Lord. (The light of the Lord will bring to understanding and remembrance shadows within the soul which hinder growth and wholeness.)   Proverbs 20:27

In what way has the Spirit of God been searching your life recently? What areas do you see needing spiritual growth?

_____

_____

    6. When person has been born again of the Spirit of God (become a Christian), that regenerated human spirit will sustain the person through their weaknesses, and infirmities. A person who is not born again does not have the strength of the Lord to bear the pain of the wounds inside the soul.   Proverbs 18:14
Psalm 147:3
Romans 5:3-5
Romans 8:35-37

What weaknesses (and infirmities) do you perceive that the Spirit of God has sustained you through, helping you to continue with day-to-day life?

_____

_____

7. Before regeneration (salvation experience), the human spirit is powerless to fight forces of darkness which have set themselves against the person's life to bring destruction.

Has your human spirit been empowered by the Spirit of Father God, through salvation? Have you been born again? (Read John 14:6. There is no other path to freedom.)

Explain your experience here.

_____

_____

_____

_____

_____

_____

<u>Kidnapped!</u>

It had been in the family for years, generations in fact.

In the old days, it had had a much stronger influence, too.

It crouched in the corner, waiting for the miner's son, now grown, to enter his bedchamber. He was most vulnerable when he was most tired. And these days, the spirit found it necessity to wait until he was exhausted. Only then did he have a chance, and it was a slight one at best.

After all, it reasoned to itself, hadn't Eden given a legal right to the Darkness? It had earned this privilege! Thinking about it, the apparition mused. Really, seeing the inroads made into the church, this should be expected.

The family had invited this, years ago.

Yes, it had a right to wait here, in the darkness.

****

Martin had not had an easy day. He had met with the leadership of the Catholic Church as they had requested him to that morning, in the city of Worms.

It hadn't been the first meeting they had had together there.

Three months prior, they had asked him to stop his work. The council actually wanted him to turn his back on the Liberty he was experiencing deep within his own soul. They wanted him to come back, willingly, to return to living his life under the oppression and scrutiny under which they themselves suffered.

Religion was a heavy burden, so full of Deception.

They had asked him to recant.

       And give up Joy;
               And Peace;
                      And, for the first time in his life, Contentment.

Deep in thought, he lit the candle in his room.

This had been a hard road; this arrival to the place of Freedom. When he was young, he had thought to become a lawyer. He felt he could best help people that way. There were so many in such deep need. They had no one to speak for them; no one to represent them in the courts.

His mother had said he had the mind for it, and Martin had found it to be true. He had studied hard.

Then, toward the end of his days at the University of Erfurt (Germany), he had discovered Life. An awakening to spiritual things had been taking place in western Europe. It had began with the students in the universities. Martin had gone to a few meetings close to the campus, and realized there was more to Church than just attending meetings and keeping the organization running.

He was shaken to the very core.

He would never forget the day he had changed his course, and set his sails with the Wind of God. He would become a priest.

Blessedly, he already knew Latin. He would learn Greek; and Hebrew if need be.

He was determined to know God.
                                        And knowing Him, to please Him.

After several years, Martin Luther had become a professor at the University at Wittenberg. The students loved him. He was one of their favorite teachers. He could explain the Heart of Abba God so that they could hold on to their understanding. He was making a difference in their lives. He wrote pamphlets to explain what he was teaching, written in the common man's language. Everyone needed to know the Father. Those writings had caused an uproar; not only among the students who were discovering life in Christ, but then among the leaders of the Catholic church around the college.

Martin began to dress for bed.

Something about the Light revealed in those pamphlets had apparently upset things in the spiritual realm. All sorts of reactions had taken place!

The devil had been intimidated by the Darkness' loss of control within the church. More than half of the people Martin had shared Truth with had received the same Liberty he had found.

Why was it so hard for people to choose the Right Road?

He shook his head. How he grieved over the friends who would not receive the Liberty of Christ.
He was surprised at the emotion rising up against the enemy of his soul; and their souls as well. Martin hated the devil with a Perfect hatred.

There could be no compromises.

They had declared him a heretic today.

Then, just ten hours ago, they had delivered to him a piece of paper which excommunicated him from the Catholic Church. He had burned it in public view.

Martin smiled. Rejected by men? Perhaps. But, he would be obedient to the inner nudges of the Spirit of God within him. He couldn't wait to begin his project.

And, what better time than now?

****

The demon watched him, still not moving. It was waiting for a sign of weakness or self-pity to signal the beginning of its attack. It was looking for a crack in the door of his soul.

Martin Luther had been hard to find tonight.

*******.****************************

Father God was also watching. The ministering angels He had commissioned to touch the soul of Martin Luther were doing their job well. The Spirit of God within the man, and the Revelation he had been entrusted with were intact. The Father rejoiced. He had much purpose for this man.

This moldable man.
        Martin would need the quiet.

****

Martin washed his face.

The emperor had condemned him this morning, but had allowed him to leave for home, instead of sending him directly to prison. Amazed, Martin Luther mounted his horse and began the trek to Wittenberg. He was not afraid, although there had been many plots against his life. The Peace of God was with him.

When he reached the outskirts of Eisenach, a band of masked horsemen had seized him. He thought he was about to die.

He had not been afraid.

He was ready to meet the Father. Perhaps he had accomplished his life's purpose, he reasoned. Perhaps he had just been the one the Lord desired to light the fire. Someone else would add the wood, as the Spirit breathed upon the embers.

The hooded bandits had spirited him away to a castle which belonging to a friend, Frederick, the Elector of Saxony. Upon his arrival, Frederick had informed Martin that for all practical purposes Martin would be a prisoner in the castle until the spiritual climate of the country was right for the next move in the Plan of God.

Martin dried his face, and brushed his hair.

****

The demon felt a presence next to it. Looking over, it shriveled away in fear and disgust. Why was the master of the Darkness here in person? Without a word, Satan dismissed the spirit to another task.

This job had become a priority.

****

Ready for rest, and looking forward to the plans of Abba Father had designed for his life the next morning, Luther knelt down by the bed to speak with his Father; his Creator; the Restorer of his soul.

Satan spoke. "You are a sinner, Martin Luther."

Luther continued to pray. He shut his eyes to shut out the distractions beating against his soul.

The whisperer continued. "Did God *really* tell you to divide the church? You are one of those who revile against other men, Martin. You are a heretic. There is no hope for you. Perhaps you could have earned forgiveness for your sins before, but now there is no shred of grace. It is too late. You have gone too far."

Luther opened his eyes and looked into the corner. The Spirit of the Father within him spoke into the darkness.

"Look at your own sins, old fellow. Get out of here. The Blood of Jesus is against you."

Satan could feel the heat of the consuming fire of the Holy Spirit which raged within this man. He could also feel the Blood of the Lamb melting the wall of indecision and confusion he had taken so long to prepare and bring with him.

He fled as fast as he could.

                                                          But he would be back.

The Peace of the Almighty filled the room. God's goodness overwhelmed him, as he slipped into the covers.

But he was too full of joy to sleep!! Suddenly, Martin's mind could hardly keep up with the Understanding!! It was almost too much!!

Martin Luther arose, lit another candle, and began to translate the New Testament from Greek into German.

> **Please listen to the sixth CD, utilizing your notebook, for Session Six**
>
> **"The Problem with Pride, Deception, and Spiritual Imprinting"**
> **before you move ahead**

<u>**Notes:**</u>

The Soul of Man
"The soul that sins; it shall die." Ezekiel 18:4

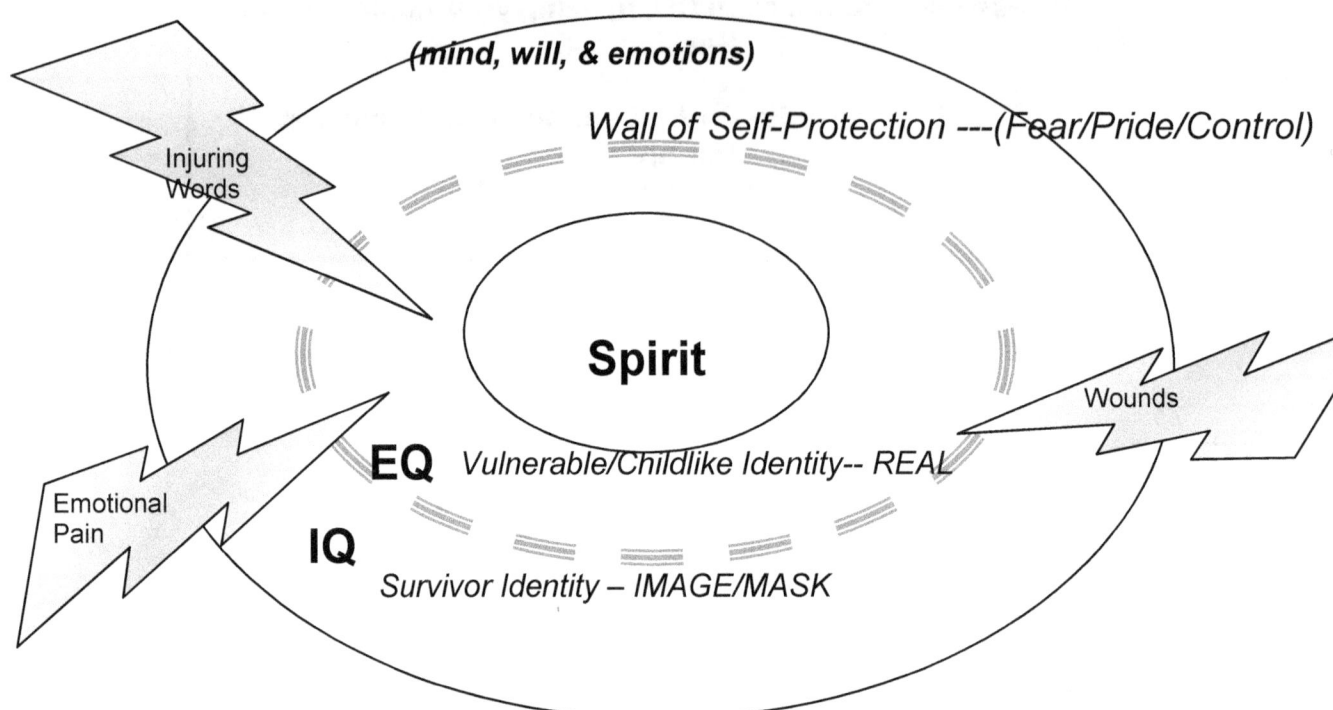

Problem: The soul of man carries the consequences of the willful choice made in Eden. The ingesting of the fruit allowed the poison of Satan's disposition to permeate every area of the personality. The natural tendencies of the human soul changed from likeness of Father God (in His image), to those of Satan himself.

Solution: The soul must be transformed by the same explosive power which regenerated the spirit of man. A willful choice must be made in every area of the soul, turning the heart toward the likeness of Father God. Each area of the mind, the will and the emotions must be surrendered to the Will and Plan of God by the willful choice of man. 'We must realize that it is Satan's desire that we repeat the process of Eden's fall on a daily basis, ignoring our weaknesses, and hiding our sin from the all-seeing eyes of Father God.

> By the memorized and applied Word of God --we must forcibly choose to align our belief systems with what the Word of God says -and *only* what the Word of God says. We cannot lean on experiences or traditions.

Observation: Eve's sin came through deception. She actually believed that she was doing the right thing –that somehow her actions were bring her closer to God. Adam's sin was willful and deliberate. He knew and remembered exactly what Father God had said, but chose to follow his wife's example, buying into the lies of rebellion. (See I Timothy 2:14, I Corinthians 15:22, and Romans 10:12) Both types of sin bring death. One is not less destructive than the other.

Principle: Confession brings Covering (I John 1:9, Genesis 3:8-12 and 21)

Fragmented Areas of the Human Soul

1. **Vulnerable Personhood--**
   a. promotes self interests
   b. eager to please authority, teachable
   c. relationship oriented
   d. acceptance/approval is basis for life
   e. God-created personality, compliant with God's plan
   f. is willing to wait for a reasonable time
   g. perceptions are intuitive
   h. can be bruised by rejection, abandonment, abuse

Circle those descriptions in "The Will to Be Obedient" with which you see identification in your own life. Note: This part of the soul, often called the "inner child," is the most vulnerable part of a person's identity.

2. **Survivor Personhood --**
   a. promotes self-interests
   b. stubborn, self-reliant
   c. rule oriented
   d. appearance/status is basis for life
   e. Task and Image-created personality
   f. demands gratification of desires; immediate satisfaction
   g. perceptions are based upon pride and reputation
   h. capable and independent, "in control", "I will survive", "I will prove myself"

Circle those descriptions in "The Self-Will" with which you see identification in your own life. Note: This part of the soul, many times referred to as the "false self," or "projected adult," is constructed to protect fragile places of the life where wounding has occurred. (*No one has ever built a wall to protect his or her strengths.*)

It is important that we make note here that a person can be born with a walled-in fortress of Pride, from generational practices. The Wall of Self-Protection acts as a reflective mirror within the life. It gives a false sense of security, communicating that one's personality, acceptance and reputation are based upon standards put upon the life outwardly. For true growth and health to occur, a person must learn to live from the sense of security from within, based upon the deeply perceived understanding of Abba Father's acceptance and approval. These become the life lessons, and convictions for the foundation of living.

A person who lives with a fortress of Pride, lives life seeking to please his peers, afraid of rejection or disapproval, shame based, seeking to fit in with the "herd", rather than having the strength to stand for his own convictions. Fear and Rejection work as fuel for the Wall of Pride.

Qualities of the Human Soul

The Wall of Self-Protection, (usually constructed with some degree of Pride)

In its simplest definition, the quality of Pride is defined as:

> "The inability or unwillingness to trust God to take care of us; the choice to trust ourselves."

The wall of Pride then, becomes a wall of self-protection within the life of a person, separating that person from the love and care of Abba Father. It acts as a barrier between a person's inner understanding and Father God. It reflects the expectations of the world, and of other people into the soul, causing a person to construct their own identity. It requires perfection without a Perfect God. It requires righteousness without grace. In essence, it is man trying to re-create himself into the image of God --without God. Pride causes man to hide, his pain, or even deny that it exists, with emotional "fig leaves", sewn together with his own ability. Accomplishments become the validation of the life, instead of a relationship with Father God validating the life.

Pride also justifies its behavior, based upon the behavior of others. It compares itself with itself—
II Corinthians 10:12 says that this destroys Godly wisdom within the soul.
So what does the wall of pride represent?

1. It is an evidence Lucifer's rebellion against Father God.	Isaiah 14:12-15
2. It is a fruit of the sin of Adam in the garden of Eden.	Mark 7:22 I Timothy 6:3-4 James 4:6 I Peter 5:5
3. It shuts up the heart. (The allegorical picture is given of Leviathan, the dragon, whose scales are his pride, sealing his skin from anything which would pierce through.	Job 41:15 and 34
4. It is deceptive. The person thinks they are all right -- even exalted.	Isaiah 28:1-3 Isaiah 16:6 Obadiah 3
5. It disregards the needy.	Ezekiel 16:49
6. It hardens the mind.	Daniel 5:20
7. It can only know God from a distance.	Psalm 138:6
8. It is contentious, and stirs up strife.	Proverbs 13:10 Proverbs 28:25

9. It is impatient.   Ecclesiastes 7:8

10. It is scornful and full of contempt.   Psalm 123:4
It does not believe it must obey Jesus Christ   I Timothy 6:3-4

11. It is the basic reason for alcoholism.   Habakkuk 2:5
It is also why a drinker doesn't come home.
(When a person struggles with this, or any *They have believed a lie in some*
addiction, it is because they do not want to *area of their lives in regard to how*
admit they need to come to Father God for help, *Father God feels about them.)*
but are convinced it would be better to handle
their pain themselves.

12. It will not come into alignment with God-   James 4:6
given authorities. In doing so, it resists God,   I Peter 5:5
and will not humble itself   (II Peter 2:10)
     (Titus 3:1)

13. It is accompanied by shame   Proverbs 11:2
     Psalm 119:78

14. It is accompanied by cursing and lying.   Psalm 59:12

15. It is accompanied by a haughtiness in countenance,   Psalm 10:4
and thoughts.   Jeremiah 48:29

16. Pride is a bondage, encircling the personality   Psalm 73:6
as a chain, eventually causing violent behavior.   Isaiah 28: 1-5
It also crowns the life –meaning it provides the person
with a false identity. (Our identity as believers, our crown,
is the glory of Father God.)

What areas of your life have been affected by a wall of pride? Write them here.

_____

_____

Write out a prayer to Father God here, repenting for being influenced by pride. Renounce every place where you have allowed Pride to rule you. Submit to Father God and come under His love and protection. (James 4:7-8)

_____

_____

An overview of the Wall of Pride -- a. barrier between real person and relationships
        b. reflects expectations of the world and other people
        c. speaks a false identity
        d. demands perfection without God
        e. demands righteousness without Grace of God
        f. resists and opposes (accuses) authority figures
        g. never admits or confesses need (blindness), but has answer for others' needs
        h. driving accomplishments are the validation of life, rather than obedience and dependence on Father God.

Circle those descriptions in "The Wall of Pride" you can identify as existing within your own life.

_____

_____

It is important that we make note here that a person can be born with a walled-in fortress of Pride, from generational practices. The wall of pride acts as a reflective mirror within the life. It gives a false sense of security, in that one~ personality, acceptance and reputation are based upon standards which have been put upon the life outwardly, rather than from God-given standards, based upon inner convictions within the soul. A person who lives with a fortress of Pride, lives life to suit his peers, seeking to fit in with the "herd", rather than having the strength to stand for his own convictions. Fear and Rejection work as fuel for the Wall of Pride.

Pride also justifies its behavior, based upon the behavior of others. It compares itself with itself --II Corinthians 10:12 says that this destroys Godly wisdom within the soul.

Write out a prayer of confession here, acknowledging your need of Father God's intervention and help in healing your will here. Repent for accommodating Pride, and for seeking to construct your own identity, based on the identity you thought you were supposed to portray, from the expectations and pressures of other people; as well as circumstances and events in your life history.

_____

_____

_____

_____

Contemplation

It had been a beautiful place.

He had had the chance to name each animal himself. Each one was so different...

And the garden... ...it was full of delightful fruits. How had Father conceived of so many different varieties? Each type had tasted differently. What a wonderful location it had been!

There had been no Pain.

"Ouch!" Adam shook his finger, and quickly put the cut thumb in his mouth. Where had that stone come from? He stopped his cultivating and looked out over the desert in front of him. Eden had been such a Paradise! How could he have given it all away?

There had been no Fear.

It was his own fault. He knew that now. Eve had thought her choice really was the right one. He could have stopped her. After all, Abba Father had originally created the garden to be his responsibility. She had been placed into his care as well.

The serpent had been so easy to believe... ...He had known how to twist what Father God had told them. He had even *seemed* like a friend. Adam could not blame Eve for being deceived... ...but his own choice? He remembered the moment. His choice had been deliberate.

His curiosity had cost him everything.

Had life really been the best it could be?

What a foolish question!!

Adam went back to working the ground with renewed vigor. He had to get these plants in if they wanted to eat. The boys were eating more these days.

"I traded it all away for a piece of fruit." He was talking to himself now. "We didn't have to worry about anything. Father God was everything to us --even clothing. And now... ..." he stopped to wipe the beads of sweat from his face before they fell into his eyes.

He would never forget the look on her face when he had obeyed Fear. "It was the woman You gave me – she did it. It was *her* fault. *I* didn't do anything, God." It hadn't even been "Abba," or "Father" – just "God."

But he *had* done something. Adam had chosen, knowing the consequences. Why had he blamed her? They had talked it out so many times since that day --

                                    still the question always haunted him..

He reached for the next plant, and placed its tiny roots into the soil. This job had been easier in Eden, too. Why hadn't he just been honest with Father? Why had he listened to Pride?

Pride had told him to cover himself; to hide the nakedness of his sin. To keep secret his newly found weakness.
           And Shame ….   nothing would ever be good enough again.

      He would never have the confidence of being whole and complete again;

not without sacrifice, and the shedding of blood. The fruit had forfeited the eternal quality they had carried – the Light and Life of Abba's throne. Father God had covered them before they had to leave Eden. And now, if he wanted to get rid of this awful pain in his soul, he had to make a sacrifice.

Now, his soul was desperately hungry for what he had known before –
                      But his appetites drew him in the opposite direction.

It was as though the serpent ruled his cravings – and the cravings of his sons – and Eve as well.

That eternal sense of destiny had died as well. Oh, there were moments when he sensed it again – fleetingly, as though it were in the morning mist – but it had never been the same. It was just a distant memory – something valuable he had to work to discover over and over again.

Well, he thought. The knowledge carried in the fruit they had eaten had done the deed. Adam knew that now as well. Why was his hindsight always better than his foresight? Knowledge without perception, information without understanding, truth without application – all of these could kill the inner part of a man.

And now? He arched his back to deal with the aching pain from bending over so long -- he had eaten the fruit that had poisoned his generation's blood, and every generation's blood after him; poisoned with sin --and with death.

Abba Father had said a day would come when He would make things right again. Adam held on to that... ...

He began digging the next furrow for the bean plants.

> *"And not only this, but we also joy in God through our Lord Jesus Christ, through whom we have received the atonement. Therefore, just as through one man sin entered into the world, and death through sin, and so death spread to all men, because all sinned...*
>
> *For as through the one man's disobedience the many were made sinners, even so through the obedience of the One, the many will be made righteous." Romans 5:11-12 and 19*

The Reinforcement of the Wall of Pride

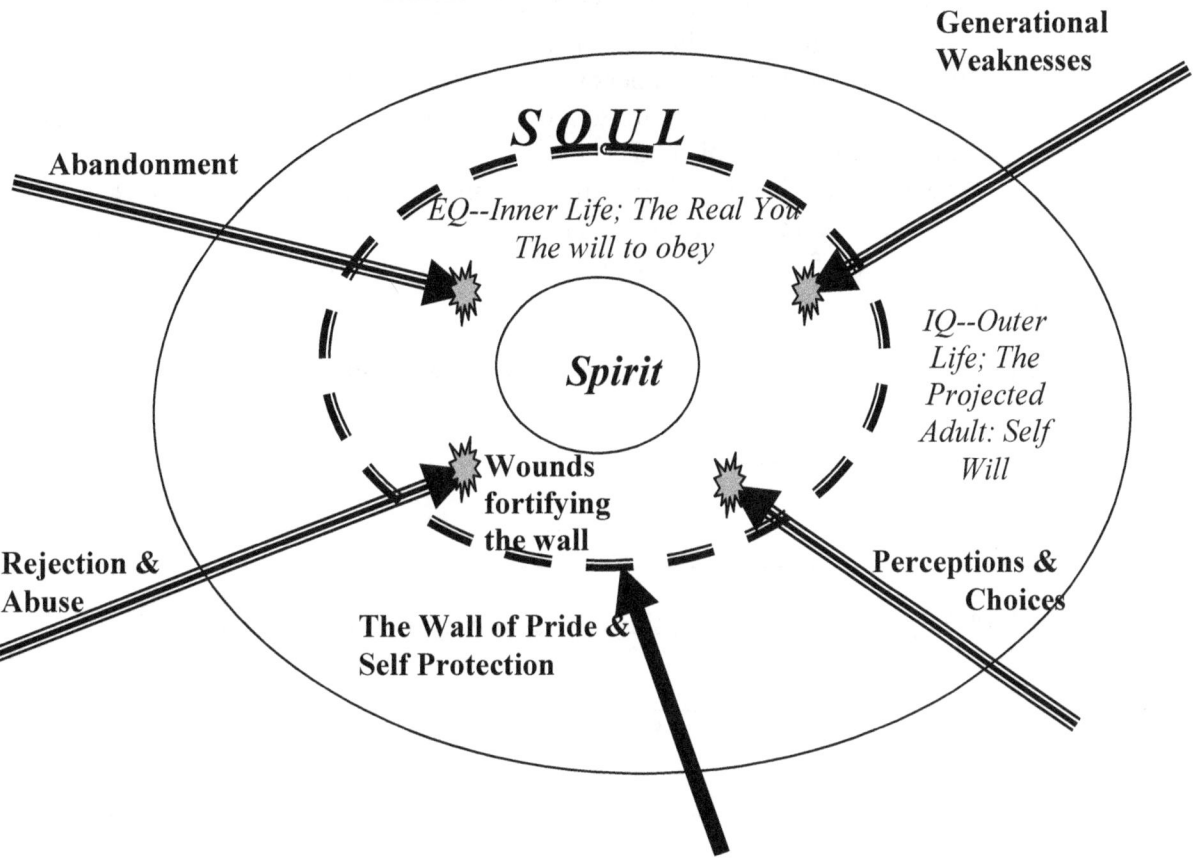

1. Abandonment -- Defined as physical abandonment; Emotional abandonment through neglect; Abandonment in growth process due to lack of communication and/or involvement during critical years; the provision of a non-biblical role model or example; the failure of a parent or authority figure to provide support, protection, or communication during a crucial time of development, or during a time of trauma; the departing parent in a divorce is perceived by the child as abandoning the child.

In what ways has a wall of pride within your own soul been reinforced due to abandonment in your life?

_____

_____

Read Hebrews 13:5. What promise has Father God made to you in this Scripture?

_____

2. Rejection-- It is defined as: the disallowance or denial of a person's worth or value; Emotional rejection through unrealistic expectations; Violation of trust by an authority figure within a person's trust system; betrayal; taunts heard and perceived as truth in regard to a person's characteristics and demeanor. The absence of communicated acceptance and affirmation during times of development by an authority figure; can be brought on be a person's perceptions as well as by actual events; perfectionist standards communicate rejection of a child's incomplete abilities to perform.

How has Rejection contributed to reinforcing a wall of pride in your own life?

_____

_____

Read Isaiah 41:9-10. What promise has Father God made to you in this Scripture?

_____

_____

2b. Abuse -- **It is defined as:** Physical or emotional violation of the soul of a person, through sexual perversion, verbal tirades, or physical blows. Threats of blows or undeserved and unrealistic punishment; Being the brunt of another person's unjust anger; Being forced to do something against your will, with threat of danger without compliance.

In what ways have you shut your heart off from vulnerability due to abuse in your life?

_____

_____

Read Psalm 145:8-9. What is the character or Father God toward you? Will He abuse or violate you? Based on what you know or His nature, can you believe His Word?

_____

_____

4. Generational Weaknesses -- These are those tendencies and appetites which have been passed from one generation to another. Addictions, illnesses, and dependencies which "run in the family".

What generational weaknesses "run" in your family?

_____

_____

Read Exodus 34:7, Numbers 14:18, and Deuteronomy 5:9. What generational sins could you be carrying in your life, which would affect your ability to become totally free in your soul?

_____

_____

5. The Reinforced Well of Pride: We cling to this wall for self preservation. When a person has been wounded within the soul, a decision is made, whether Consciously, or subconsciously. "I will not allow myself to be hurt like that again. I will take care of myself. I will not relinquish control of my life again --to anyone." This reinforced wall of pride is actually an open door to demonic forces, inviting a controlling spirit to rule the will, which in turn rules the life.

In what ways have you taken control of your life, seeking to prevent the repetition of hurts and bruises upon your soul? (If you can recall a specific instance, write it down).

_____

_____

Note: On the next two pages is a suggested prayer, to help you to begin the process of freedom from things passed down from your preceding generations. Be aware that if you are from a blended family, or if you were adopted, you will have more than one family line needing to be addressed.

A Prayer to Help in Overcoming Generational Ties

*"I the Lord am a jealous God, visiting the iniquity of the fathers
upon the children unto the third and fourth generation
of them that hate me."* Deuteronomy 5: 9

A generational tie is a link existing in the spiritual and emotional realm between a parent and child. Many bondages and tendencies, such as alcoholism and addictive behaviors are passed from one generation to the next. These generational ties provide a weak spot in the emotional make-up of a person; which the enemy then uses to inflict pain and temptation. Generational ties must be cut off through prayer and confession, and the person must willfully link their heritage to their Heavenly Father, the only Perfect Parent, their God and Redeemer.

Three things tie us to generational sin.
Each one must be confronted and broken.

1. Generational heritage (Numbers 14:18)
2. Words we have spoken (proverbs 6:2)
3. Unforgiveness (Mark 11:25-26)

Father God, I acknowledge You as my heavenly Father.
I choose to submit my life to you, In every area of my spirit,
my soul and my body. I want to be obedient to Your will.

I love and honor your Son, Jesus Christ who died for me.
I want to follow in His steps.

I repent for any sin, known or unknown, which I have committed,
that would give the devil a legal reason to keep this generational tie in my life.

I renounce the generational sins of *my* forefathers,
biological and adopted. I repent and renounce, all sexual sin,
all perversion, all witchcraft, all addictions.

I repent and renounce every place and instance where
comfort and escape were sought after in substitution for Your Presence

I choose to break the inherited iniquities from my
forefathers within my life. I will only pass on your nature and your life
to my succeeding generations.

I break every soul tie, every hex, every spell, every curse,
every sacrifice, every blood sacrifice, every voodoo,
and every work of darkness set against
my life because of generational sin.

I plead the Blood of Jesus over these areas of bondage.
I choose to align my heritage with You, Father God.
I am Your child. I choose Your way.

> **Please listen to the seventh CD, utilizing your notebook, for Session Seven**
>
> **"Relational Basics and the Religious Spirit"**
> **before you move ahead**

Notes:

Characteristics of the Reinforced Wall of Pride

1. Generational tendencies are not only passed down from one generation to another, but they also become part of a person's personality description due to role models, environment and habit patterns. These ingrained lifestyles can make change difficult to pursue. However, nothing is stronger than an engaged will, empowered by the Spirit of God to change. The weapons for warfare are found in the Word of God. The more a person memorizes of the Word of God, and seeks to apply that Word to his or her daily lifestyle and character, the more territory within the soul will be gained in spiritual and emotional freedom.

Read Proverbs 25:28. Write it out <u>here.</u>

_____

_____

2. In the book of Nehemiah, the historical account is given of the rebuilding of the walls of the city of Jerusalem. As a capital city, Jerusalem represented the identity of the nation of Israel at that time. Its walls had been destroyed and its gates burned by king Nebuchadnezzar of Babylon. As a nation, Israel had no identity of its own. By the same token, as a city, Jerusalem had no identity of her own, either. Jerusalem's enemies could come and go into the city at will, because there were no fortified walls to protect her.

In Isaiah 22:9-11, a description is found of the actions of the people in Jerusalem when they discovered that the walls were broken down. Read these verses and then write out verses 10-11 here.

_____

_____

3. A house is a place of habitation; a dwelling place. It is interesting that the places where Jerusalem really lived were destroyed in order to fortify a wall, which in essence was constructed of an accumulation of bits and pieces of leftover trash. Anything to protect the identity of the city and, in a sense, provide a false identity and sense of security.

In the same way, the wall of pride within the soul is made up of the forsaken dreams and goals of a person's real identity. Many times, in order to satisfy the demands for a false self --whether put upon the person from outward sources, or from perceptions from within --a person will "tear down" God-given hopes and dreams for their life in the effort to satisfy an image they feel they must portray. The wall, or identity, they portray is a false self, made up of the wall of pride.

Behind the wall, the real person, many times bruised and emotionally crippled, waits for the Father's love to break through and release them from the bondages of Pride and Shame.

In what ways have you "torn down" God-given dreams and desires within your own life, and allowed Pride to build a wall to give you identity?

_____

_____

4. In Nehemiah 1:3, is a description of the walls of Jerusalem. The gates, or entryways of the city had been burned with fire by Nebuchadnezzar. In Bible times, ruling decisions were made at the gates of a city (Proverbs 31:23, Ruth 4: 1,11). The gates were also a symbol a city's authority and protection in an area or province of a country (Matthew 16:18, Judges 16:1-4).

The fact that Jerusalem's gates were burned meant that both her ability to make decisions as a nation, as well as her authority over the territory in which she dwelt would have to be rebuilt from fresh materials. *(It is interesting to note that the meaning of the Hebrew name "Nehemiah", is Comforter --The ministry of Nehemiah in helping Jerusalem to rebuild the walls of her identity, is the ministry of the Holy Spirit within the lives of each of us today.)*

In what areas of your life do you have difficulty making decisions?

_____

_____

In what areas of your life do you feel you cannot stand confidently without help?

_____

_____

Bible Words For Pride

There are several words used within the Hebrew and Greek languages, which have varying meanings, all of which have been translated as simply "pride", when put into English.

1. "Ga'own" --Hebrew

(meaning: pride, pomp, swelling, arrogancy, proud, excellency, majesty)

When it is used in a good sense, this word describes the majesty and glory of Almighty God, for all glory and recognition belongs to Him. (Is. 24:14, Is 60:15)

When it is used in a negative sense, this word describes the self-recognition and advancement which pride bestows upon the soul, without regard to the actual Source of True Glory and Power, Father God. Self is given the credit for achievements, accomplishments, and abilities. God hates this character trait, and promises to break its strength.

(Lev. 26:19, Proverbs 8:13, Proverbs 16:18, Isaiah 13:11, Isaiah 23:9, Ezek. 7:24, Ezek. 16:39, Ezek. 30:6)

Are there ways you have allowed pride to seduce and deceive you into taking credit for gifts, achievements, or abilities the Father has provided you with?

_____

_____

2. "Zadown" --Hebrew (meaning: presumptuous, arrogance, insolence)

To be insulting, and/or grossly lacking in respect for authority, whether in attitude or action. A brash, bold and excessive self-confidence. To be disdainful or haughty in behavior or appearance. It is accompanied by shame and contention (Proverbs 11:2 and 13:10). The fruit of its presence is deception and the desire to "see and be seen" (Jeremiah 49: 16). It cannot help but show itself when it is fully developed, in violence, thus drawing the judgment of God. (Ezekiel 7:9-11)

Do you struggle with shame over some of the areas of your life? _____

Are there areas of your life where you have allowed Pride to shield those areas of hurt, by becoming hard-hearted?

_____

_____

3. **"Gobahh" --Hebrew**

(meaning: haughtiness, loftiness, exaltation, grandeur)

To exalt oneself in position above all, in order to "oversee". The desire to "know all, and see all." The feeling that it is one's right to be above certain responsibilities and places of service. (II Chronicles 32:26) The refusal to seek after the Lord --even to the point of developing a haughty look (Psalm 10:4) This type of pride incurs God's judgment.

What points of Christian service have you considered "too low", or have you said that you would "rather not" have to do? Are there areas of your life which have been status-focused?

_____

_____

Do you see that the desire to pursue this type of heart attitude is actually a form of pride? Write out a prayer of repentance and confession here.

_____

_____

4. **"Ge'uwth" --Hebrew**

(meaning: pride, raging, lifting up, rising up -- in regard to a column of smoke)

Describes the drunkards of Ephraim (Isaiah 28:1-3). This scripture refers to the crown (or ruling spirit) of pride, under which those who in bondage to alcohol live. Pride is accompanied by a blindness to the need or the difficulty, and a sense that one can heal oneself, without Father God's help -all that is needed is a "little escape."

Read II Corinthians 4:4. Who has blinded the eyes of those who do not believe?

Many times, the ruling reign of pride in a life is accompanied by anger and hatred, and it is usually somewhat justified. Write out I John 2:11 here.

_____

_____

5. "Rokec" --**Hebrew**

(meaning: snares, plots, conspiracy)

The Lord will hide the righteous in a secret place, where the pride (or plots and conspiracies) of Satan and of other men cannot hurt them.
This scripture also mentions the "strife of tongues". Pride always seeks to justify itself, while pointing the finger of blame elsewhere.(Psalm 31:20)

In what ways have you sought to protect yourself from receiving blame for difficulties and circumstances?

_____

_____

Do you find yourself continually seeking to justify your actions, so that you are seen to be "right"? Do you see the root of pride in this behavior?

_____

In the Mark 7:20-23, Jesus refers to Pride as an expression which defiles, or contaminates and stains, the character of a person. What other characteristics of the flesh are listed in these verses?

_____

_____

Write out I John 2:16 here.

_____

_____

Write out a prayer of repentance for those areas of your life which you have allowed yourself to be ruled by Pride here.
(Note: to repent means to turn completely away from. It is a choice rather than a feeling.)

_____

_____
_____

_____

What the Wall of Pride Looks Like

1. The Wall of Pride is reinforced through the life experiences in a person's life, or through generational visitation of family infirmities. Here are evidences of a reinforced wall of pride in a person's life.

        a. Pride causes Perfectionism   Jeremiah 17:5-11

Where would perfectionism have become part of the wall of your identity?

_____

_____

Who is responsible for perfection in your life and in your development? Read II Samuel 22:33, and Psalm 18:32.

_____

        b. Pride causes harsh words   Ephesians 4:32

Do you find yourself showing undue harshness toward others, which you cannot really explain ?_____

        c. Pride causes Insensitivity   Philippians 2:3-4
        d. Pride causes Judgment upon others   Matthew 7: 1
        e. Pride causes Criticism   Psalm 1:1

Do you have a difficult time showing mercy to those who have hurt you, or do you find yourself hurting those you love with your actions and attitudes?

_____

        f. Pride causes un-forgiveness   Matthew 6:14-15
        g. Pride incites takings Revenge   Jeremiah 17:10

Do you ever feel that "getting even" is okay? _____

Are there "some sins" that are acceptable?_____

Do you ever struggle with hatred toward anyone? _____

      h. Pride causes Driving Ambition   Psalm 118:8-9

How important is success to you?
_____

      i. Pride causes Competition   Psalm 146:3-4

Do you feel it is necessary to always be the one who is best, first, or "right"? _____

      j. Pride causes Unbelief   Hebrews 3:12

Do you have a difficult time taking God at His Word? _____

      k. Pride causes a person to become Independent,
      with no acknowledgment of need   Hebrews 3:12

Is it difficult for you to accept undeserved and unearned gifts from others, even if you have a need?

_____

      l. Pride causes Striving with God   Psalm 2:11-12

Do you struggle to surrender to Father God? In what ways is it hard for you to trust Him?

_____

      m. Pride brings the Refusing to do God's will   Psalm 40:8
                                                             Ephesians 5: 17
      n. Pride causes Obstinacy; Stubbornness   I Samuel 15:23

Have you ever been described as a stubborn, or hard-headed person? _____

In what ways is this statement true about you? _____

1. Revenge, an Evidence of Pride in the Soul

> Abba Father says not to take revenge, with the promise that if we do not take things sent to wound us personally - He will on our behalf.
>
> Leviticus 19: 18
> Proverbs 24:29

In what ways have you struggled with the desire to take revenge for a wrong you have suffered, or for a an injury received by someone you love?

_____

_____

Can you trust Father God to take your part? Write out a prayer of release here.

_____

_____

2. Trust in Self, an Evidence of Pride in the Soul

Those who trust in the flesh will come to a bad end. Jeremiah 17:1-1

In what ways do you trust yourself most to make things happen in your life, or in the lives of those around you?

_____

_____

Do you think Father God is able to satisfy your heart's deepest desires? Does He know you better than you know yourself? Write out a prayer of relinquishment of control here.

_____

_____

3. **Ambition, An Evidence** of Pride **in the Soul**

1. Lucifer's sin was his ambition to take God's place   Isaiah 14:12-15

In what ways have you been deceived by ambition in your life? What things is it possible that ambition has stolen from you?

_____

_____

Write out a prayer to Father God here. Repent for allowing these characteristics of Pride to control your life and responses. Renounce any and every hold they have had upon you. Make a decision not to be ruled by these things from this point forward, and then, Break the power they have had in your life. Then, read the prayer out loud, making confession of those places where you have allowed your heart to be ruled by the Wall of Pride.

_____

_____

4. Anger, An Evidence of Pride in the Soul   (scripture study on following pages)

> The uncontrolled expression of frustration, fear, indignation, and wrath. When held within, it is the condition of the overwhelmed soul, which cannot find solution to its pain. The heart feels a pull to satisfy responsibilities, but knows it is incapable of doing so, and becomes overwhelmed and angry. It is the flesh's response to correction. The attitude of one betrayed who feels unable to allow the heart to trust.

It is a secondary emotion, which masks hurt, disappointment, or areas emotional areas undeveloped within the soul. It is an open door to the bondage of violence and fear.

(Hebrew) "'aph" --anger which shows on the countenance and nostrils
(Hebrew) "ka'ac" --to be angry, vexed, grieved, indignant, or provoked

Are there any ways in which you have allowed anger to control you, or those around you? List them here.

_____

What Father God says regarding Anger:

      a. We are told not to be quick to anger, because it rests in the bosom of fools.   Ecclesiastes 7:9

What circumstances weaken your ability to control your anger? (What "pushes your buttons?")

_____

      b. Anger stirs up strife. Controlling anger stops that strife.   Proverbs 15:18
      c. Contention accompanies anger.   Proverbs 21:19
                                                                     Proverbs 26:21

Angry words accompany an angry heart. What hurts have you inflicted upon those around you through allowing your anger to control you?

_____

_____

      d. Postponing a sinful expression of anger is wise.   Proverbs 19:11

What circumstances defuse anger within you?

_____

_____

What could you do the next time you are angry to stop the progression of anger within your soul?

      e. The devil provokes us to become angry over how we are dealt with by Abba Father. (He accuses God.)   I Samuel 1:6-7

When you are wounded, what inner voices do you hear, provoking you to accuse Father God for your difficulty and pain? What do these voices say to you? Journal those thoughts here.

_____

   f. Anger is the root of the desire to kill.   Genesis 4:5-8
                                 II Samuel 12:5

In what ways have you felt justified in expressing your anger? Have you ever hurt someone close to you with your anger?

___

In what ways has the Wall of Pride deceived in regard to allowing anger to control you?

___

___

Examples of Uncontrolled Anger:

1. The murder of Abel   Genesis 4:5-8

2. The murder of the men of Shechem   (Genesis 34) Genesis 49:5-7

3. The beating of Balaam's donkey   Numbers 22:27-29

4. Nebuchadnezzar's judgment of three young Hebrew men.   Daniel 3:13-19

5. The stoning of Stephen   Acts 7:54-58

Lucifer's heart filled with pride when he led the rebellion against Father God in the heavenly realm. Because Adam partook of the fruit in Eden, and it became part of his being, pride now has an open door in every person born on the planet. We were all born from the seed of Adam. Therefore, we all carry sin.

On the next two pages is a suggested prayer, to help you to begin the process of freedom from Pride and its influences within your soul. Be aware that if you have developed habitual life-patterns of ambition, perfectionism, anger, etc., you will need to confront these desires and attitudes on a daily basis, applying the Word of God and prayer for liberation and continued freedom.

Note: Because the world operates according to the principle of the Pride of Life, allowing pride to rule your heart opens the door for a spirit of control to enter the life, invoking bondage. Pride is a spiritual as well as soulful problem. Allowing the heart to be ruled by Pride invites demonic activity into the life.

A Scripture-Based Prayer
To Overcome Pride
(A spirit of contention, control and self-rule)

"The fear of the Lord is to hate evil: pride, and arrogance."
Proverbs 8: 13

Pride is the basis of every sin. It is most simply seen as the "inability and unwillingness to trust God to take care of us; the insistence of taking care of ourselves." It is the expression of Satan's nature, vented through the flesh. It is the assertion of "rights", and the desire to prove ourselves to be right, at whatever cost. It is the root of self-sufficiency and independence. Its tendency is to set standards, expecting others to measure up to those standards, without first seeking God for his direction and plan. Pride means trusting in one's own abilities and strengths, and then expecting a blessing for a "good" idea.

Pride must be confronted daily in the human soul. If given any ground, the deceit of pride will gain ground in every area and render the believer useless and ineffective in prayer and in service.

Biblical Indications that Pride is ruling the life:

1. No answer to prayer when in need, the sense of being resisted by God. (James 4:6, I Peter 5:5, Psalm 138:6, Proverbs 12:3 and 16:5)
2. A persecution (disregard or indifference) for the poor (Psalm 10:2)
3. Cursing and lying. (Psalm 59:12)
4. Violence (Psalm 73:6)
5. Shame (Proverbs 11:2)
6. Contention (Proverbs 13:10)
7. Deception (Jeremiah 49:16, Obadiah 3)

Note: If you struggle with attitudes of Pride or Narcissism, it will help you to read this prayer out loud every day until you begin to gain understanding and breakthrough.

Father God, I am confronted by my own willful desires to do things my way. I confess to you the pride within my own heart. I have thought more highly of myself than I ought to think. I have allowed myself to have contentious thoughts -- thoughts arguing against those who you have placed in my life as authority figures, and mentors. I repent for the foolish words of my mouth, which have exalted my own opinions and attitudes, but have resisted humbling myself to become ready to learn and ask questions to learn.

Your Word says that you hate even a proud look. Please be the lifter of my head and the light of my countenance. I renounce every door I have opened within my soul for pride to operate and gain influence. The wicked, through pride, will not seek after You, but Lord, I desire to seek you. Please reveal and root out every prideful thing within me. I will not walk with the foot of pride, or allow pride to provoke me to anger. I cut off that influence in Jesus' name.

I humble myself before You, Lord. Remove all pride and selfish ambition from me. I repent and renounce the influences of flattery in my life. Father, please forgive me for the times I have listened to man's flattery, allowing those words to shape the image of who you desire me to be.

I only want to be what you want me to be. I repent and renounce every flattering word in the name of Jesus.

I repent and renounce every lie and deception I have practiced because of the influence of pride. With the fear of the Lord comes wisdom, but the fool is proud. It is my desire to become filled with the fear of the Lord. Keep me from falling into the trap of pride. I want to choose your ways, instead of my own ways. I cut off the chains of pride with the Blood of the Lamb.

It is my choice to cut off from my life a proud look, a haughty attitude, a lying tongue, and the sowing of conflict among the brethren. I know and understand that you hate these things. I choose to show mercy and unconditional love to everyone I come in contact with. I choose to be a peacemaker, acting like a child of my Abba Father God.

It is my choice to clothe myself with humility as with a garment, and to regard your workings in me as wondrous and miraculous. No longer will look for what I consider myself to have earned. I choose to wait upon You, Lord, for your purposes and plans for my life. I cast down every vain imagination, exalting itself against the knowledge of God in my life. I will lean only on my own abilities and knowledge for answers and understanding from this time forward.

Pride, I will not serve to express you any longer. I cut off every bud and seed of pride from growing in my life and soul. I belong to the Lord God of Hosts, and I choose to be under His authority. I will not seek to be my own authority. The Blood of the Lamb of God is against you, and is applied to the door of my life. You have no authority to speak to me, because I choose to remove every legal right I have given you to rule and influence in my life. You cannot speak into my life, or influence me, because my hope is in the Lord Jesus Christ and His work upon the Cross. I stand in the accomplished work of the Blood of Jesus. I will not give you place any longer.

Psalm 36:11	Psalm 59:12	Psalm 73:6	Proverbs 8: 3
Mark 7:22	Proverbs 14:3	Proverbs 16:18	Ezekiel 7:10
Daniel 5:20	Psalm 123:4	I John 2:16	Psalm 4:6
Psalm 12:3	Psalm 40:4	Proverbs 28:25	Proverbs 6:16-17
Proverbs 15:25	Proverbs 16:5	Proverbs 21:4	Proverbs 13:10

A Scripture-Based Prayer
To Overcome Anger, Rage and Violence

*"He that is slow to anger is better than the mighty,
and he that rules his own spirit than he that takes a city." Proverbs 16:32*

Anger is a secondary emotion. It erupts to the surface of a life when there is unresolved pain, emotional lack of development, or unforgiven hurt in a person's life. In smaller issues, anger is easily dealt with, by making a choice to forgive the person who has hurt you, and laying the right of keeping of life-accounts at the feet of Father God. In I Corinthians 13, the Word tells us that love keeps no record of wrongs, and in Romans 5:5, God has promised to shed His love abroad in our hearts. When we respond in anger, we are short-circuiting our opportunity to love a person with the love of God. We are keeping record of wrongs.

In larger issues, anger must be confronted aggressively. It is an area to which demonic forces seek to attach themselves, and it is usually accompanied by violence, fear and/or depression. This type of violent anger can usually be traced to an open door created in a person's childhood, through abuse, neglect, or poor modeling. Many times, a person in the cycle of the bondage of anger will seek to escape their inner pain by seeking refuge in alcohol, drugs, or another addictive behavior.

Anger is an emotion which must be dealt with quickly and aggressively, giving no place to the devil. It works like acid upon the human soul, quickly developing its own addictive habit patterns.

Note: If you struggle with attitudes of Anger, Rage or Violence, it will help you to read this prayer out loud every day until you begin to gain understanding and breakthrough.

Father God, I confess to you my anger. It is my choice to repent for allowing anger to develop in my heart. My wrath does not work your righteousness. I ask for your forgiveness for those places where I have sinned in my anger. Please develop within me the ability to be slow to anger.

Please give me a forgiving spirit. I choose to forgive those who have hurt me, and I bring you my heart. I understand that I must forgive, in order for your forgiveness to become fully released in my own life. Please heal my life, and release me from the cycle of the bondage of anger. I choose

to let go of my right to be angry. It is the desire of my heart to be able to have Holy Spirit-led control over my own spirit.

I acknowledge that Your Word says that vengeance is Yours and You will repay. I choose not to take these hurts personally, but to recognize that those who have hurt me are operating out of their own pain and bondage. In making this choice, I understand that your Word says that You will undertake in these things on my behalf. I will wait for your timing in making these things right. Thank you for loving me.

Father God, it is my choice to humble myself before You, and to allow you to rebuild the walls of my soul and personality. Anger is not the definition of your purpose for my life. Please make me what you want me to be. I choose to yield to you. Please develop the Holy Spirit's fruit of unconditional love, gentleness and kindness in my heart.

I choose to seek Your Will and Way for my life. I open the door of my soul to your love for me. Please wash away everything that stands in the way of my receiving your perfect and unconditional love.

Lord, I confess that Your Word says that my wrath does not work your righteousness. I confess that anger rests in the bosom of fools. It is my desire to be wise in every area of my life. Therefore, I choose to turn away from anger.

Anger, I will not serve you any longer. Rage, you have no hold on me. Violence, I will not be your slave. I belong to the Lord God of Hosts. The Blood of the Lamb of God is against you. I apply it to the door of my life. You have no authority to speak to me, because I choose to remove every legal right I have given you to deal in my life. Anger, you cannot speak into my life, or influence me, because my hope is in the Lord Jesus Christ and His work upon the Cross. I do not even have to fight this battle, for the battle is not mine, but it belongs to the Lord. You have been defeated by the death and resurrection of the Son of God, and I will not give you place any longer.

Proverbs 16:32	Proverbs 19:11	Proverbs 25:28	Proverbs 29:22-23
Ecclesiastes 7:9	Ephesians 4:26-27	Ephesians 4:31-32	James 1:19-20
Romans 12:19	Proverbs 15:1		

> **Please listen to the eighth CD, utilizing your notebook, for Session Eight**
>
> **"Forgiveness and Torment"**
> **before you move ahead**

Notes:

A New Beginning

The girl screamed and picked up the tray of food. She flung it at the nurse, who scurried out of the room as fast as her feet could carry her. How could they let the child live like this? How much longer could her father keep her out of the institution? She was mental. There was no doubt.

The nurse, one of a long line of medicals, handed in her resignation that very hour. She would not be back.

The skeletal, naked, human form charged at the door, with unexplainable strength and venom, clawing and scraping until her fingers bled, and her head was bruised from self-inflicted blows against the wall. Her screams of fear were punctuated with animal-like sounds, too deep for a girl her size.

"Get them off of me!" she yelled. "Can't you see them?"

"Let me out of here!"

The four hired men, who stood at her bedroom door to guard it -- to physically subdue her should she break the door down, looked at each other in fear. They would have to go in again and keep her from hurting herself.

She was only seventeen years old.

****

The letter had arrived early that morning. He had wept when he read it, and then handed it to Alice, his daughter. She looked at him.

"But Father, we receive many letters like this. Are you sure you need to go?"

"I will explain it later to you, sweetheart. I must follow the urgency of the Holy Spirit's leading in this matter. I must go."

He was a man whose heart was consumed with knowing the Abba Father. He read a "bit" from the Word of God continually; at, or close to the stroke of every fifteen minutes. It was the only Book he ever read. He was accustomed to fasting. Moreover, it was not unusual for him to break into loud "Hallelujahs!"

Even in strange, crowded, public settings.

It had become his obsession to become filled with the nature of the Spirit of God.

He bid Alice good-bye, and stepped down the porch steps of his home. He opened the car door and started the engine.

Smith thought back over his life during the journey. How had the Father chosen him? He hadn't even gone to school! From an extremely poor family, he had learned to work hard in his early years. He had learned to be thankful for everything with which he had been blessed. He and his two brothers, along with his mother and one sister had worked next to their father from their early years to provide a roof and enough food to feed the family.

He could not remember a time when he hadn't yearned for Father God. Many times, when picking turnips alongside his family members, Smith had knelt and asked God for help. His parents, though unsaved, had loved and supported him in his quest. But back then, he hadn't really known the Father yet.

He had worked in a factory since he was seven years old.

His wife had taught him to read --in his mid-twenties.

His grandmother had taken him to the Wesleyan church. He could remember the meeting when he had first discovered the Liberty of the Spirit of God. In the midst of joyous worship, people danced and sang with all their hearts to their Loving Creator. It had developed inside him a hunger for more.

Always more.

It was here Smith had learned to pray. It was here as well that he was freed from the inability to express himself. He had found it difficult to give testimony of God's goodness to him. In loving concern, three of the older men in the church had laid hands upon him and prayed. The difficulty had lifted almost immediately!

> He had never doubted his salvation since.

There had been times, though, when, after losing a battle within his soul, he had feared not being ready when Jesus returned. He had feared being left behind.

> It was the struggle with that fear which had exposed the inner battle to his eyes.

He had determined to bring his soul into obedience to the Father. He would fill his heart so full of the Word of God that there would be no room for anything else.

The car rounded the corner. The house was in sight.

****

Satan moaned in his dark place of concealment. Would it never end? It seemed that there was a man of God on every corner these days!!

And they were ruining his chances of unquestionable authority!!

They prayed like warriors. They restrained their fleshly appetites. They kept the Light of Father God alive --not just alive, but growing --within their re-born spirit beings. Worst of all, they knew his mission. They understood his purpose and his rebellion --

They treated him with the same authority, which had accompanied God on earth!

They spoke to his underlings. It was the beginning of the end. The rebellion was doomed!

>It was frightening!
>>It wasn't fair!
>>>How could it even be possible?

Wasn't Torment his legal right? Yes. He had taken control in Eden.

This invasion into his territory was inexcusable!!! Something would have to be done! And soon!

He would not go down without a fight!!

****

The Spirit of the Lord hovered just above the girl. So many had been praying for her to be set free. So many remembered the child's potential.

She needed to be free, to grow into all the Father wanted her to become.

Inside her being, the demons harassed her. They berated her and held her captive, quiet and full of fear. She could not express herself. She could not feed herself. She could not do anything she wished to do. The spirits told her she was powerless; and she believed them.

>But in truth --- they were not stronger than her will.

>>And she wanted to be free.

>>>More than anything!!

And now, within, she could see them. The biggest one turned his glowing eyes at her.

"You belong to us, now. We have a legal right to be here. Don't ever even think those thoughts of having a different life. If you even move that direction, something terrible will happen. We'll destroy you and make you pay for thinking those thoughts!"

> It is Satan's nature to hate, to enslave and to destroy anything that reminds him of the image of Father God. He hates mankind, and is indifferent to anything other than his own purposes. He is the essence of hatred and fear.

He hated her.

The girl shrunk further down -- into silence.

****

The wealthy and distinguished gentleman who opened the door had a deeply sad shadow over his countenance. His eyes looked questioningly at the caller.

"I'm Wigglesworth. I got your letter."

"Oh, come in. Please. Do come in." The bereaved father took Smith by the arm, and together they walked through the palatial and luxurious surrounding afforded by all that money could buy. They never spoke a word. Both knew the errand about to be fulfilled.

At the top of the stairs, the father opened the bedroom door, indicating that the man of God should enter. He then closed the door --

He did not go in.
He *could* not go in.

> Pain had taken its hold upon his soul.

Smith Wigglesworth, the man of God, looked at the form before his eyes. Four strong men were trying to hold her down, but could not. He moved over to where she was, and looked into her eyes. They rolled, but she could not speak. He was reminded of the man who ran to Jesus from out of the tombs, and as soon he got to Jesus, the demon powers spoke.

Suddenly, the demons indicated they were aware of Smith's presence in the room. She ceased her raging. With a venomous glare, they spat, "I know you. You are Wigglesworth, the servant of the Most High God. You can't cast us out. We are many."

The demons backed away into the far corner of the room. Smith followed. They looked at him. "She is ours."

Smith's heart was flooded with compassion for the girl, and with a holy hatred of these demons.

The Spirit of Jesus filled his heart. The Savior had come to set the captives free!!

"I'm not here to argue with you, you foul spirits. The Blood of Jesus Christ is against you. In the name of Jesus Christ, and in the power of His Resurrection, you come out of her now, and trouble her no more." Then, with a hideous scream, the announcement of their protest and exit, she was delivered.

It was as though she had awakened from a dream. Suddenly, her inner room empty, she was aware. They were gone --and so was the fear!! There was no more chatter in her head!! She didn't feel the need to hide any longer…

She smiled, a peace she had never known before exuding from her eyes. Then she looked down. She was naked!! The young woman ran from the room. Two of the hired men, aware of their duty to their employer, began to follow her, concerned for her welfare, but Smith stopped them. He explained what had happened in the spiritual, and subsequently physical realms.

It was an hour or so later, when a lighthearted set of footsteps was heard upon the stairs. She had emerged from her bedroom, totally clothed and in her right mind. Wigglesworth shared a meal with her family that afternoon, and communion the next morning with one of the sweetest girls he could ever imagine meeting.

Upon arriving home, he hugged his own daughter. "How wonderful Jesus is!" was all he said.

****

Not too many nights later, well past midnight, in the wee hours of the morning, Smith Wigglesworth was startled to awake.

He lay in his bed, wondering why the Father could have called him. He began to pray. Instantly, as he entered into the spiritual realm through prayer, he was aware of another presence --an evil presence --in the room, close to where he was.

He turned his head.

Two venomous, hate-filled eyes, glowed with evil.

Their attention was fastened upon him.

Filled with the Spirit of God, and knowing his enemy, Smith turned over onto his side, and allowed his back to face this manifested spiritual enemy.

"Oh, it's only you. " he said.

Smith slept the rest of the night like a log.

The Earthly Tent of Man – The Vessel
The Body

*"What? Know ye not that your body is the temple of the
Holy Ghost which is in you, which ye have
of God, and ye are not your own?" I Corinthians* 6: 19

Problem: The earthly tent, the body of man, wears the effects of the willful choice made in the Garden of Eden. It is subject to the destructive forces of sin, sickness and decay -- The Law of Sin and Death. (Romans 8: 1-2)

Solution: On this earth, the healing power available through the shed Blood of Jesus Christ will bring freedom as it is appropriated through our belief and surrender to His ways and purposes. On the new earth, the bodies of those who have been spiritually regenerated will be glorified and given evidence of the eternal life their spirits have received.

Principle: We must choose Christ and His Blood in order to be free. Every sickness, disease, and ill has it's roots in Lucifer's rebellion. As we grow in grace and in faith, surrendering more and more of the soul to Father God's rule, the power of the Spirit of God grows within the soul to empower us to believe for physical healing and wholeness.

Application: The Body is the vehicle for the expression of the soul of man. It is also the temple, or the place of habitation for the Spirit of God. Therefore, it must be cared for and maintained in order to best promote and express the Life and Love of Father God.

How Inner Freedom Affects the Physical Body

"Beloved, I would that you would prosper and be in health, even as your soul prospers." III John 2

1. John 13:8   If Jesus does not wash us,   (wash=Grk. "nipto"
(see Ephesians 5:26)   we have no part with Him.   to cleanse

Principle: Only Jesus can make us clean, in spirit, soul and body.

In what areas of your life do you need His cleansing?

_____

_____

Write out Ephesians 5:26 here.

_____

_____

The Word of God cleanses us when we apply its truth to our personal lives and allow our hearts and wills to come into alignment with God's ways. Memorization of the Word of God is an essential element in this cleansing.

2. John 20:26-29   We do not have to physically   (see=Grk."eido" to know by sight.
                        see in order to believe.   To perceive

                                                              believe=Grk. "pisteuo", to commit,
                                                              to put trust in, to have confidence in)

Principle: Man has the ability to believe God without depending upon his physical senses. Jesus said there was greater blessing in this type of belief.

It is a quality of Pride to demand proof before we believe. In what areas of your life have you demanded proof of Father God's love and care for you? (He already gave it at the Cross).

_____

_____

Write out a prayer of repentance here, for demanding to put belief on your own terms.

_____

_____

   3. Matthew 9:18-19   Jesus has the power to raise the dead.   (asleep=Grk
      Matthew 9:24-26   (Read John 11)   "katheudo", to sleep
                                                                                                       normally)

Principle: In the Father's perspective, death is simply a form of sleep, and should not be feared.

What things should we fear more than death? What kind of perspective does this give you in regard to the battle for inner freedom?

_____

Can opening your heart to trust Jesus' power to heal your life bring things which were had given up on back to life within you? Are you willing to trust Him? Write out a short prayer of commitment here.

_____

_____

(Remember the little boy who gave Jesus his lunch. Jesus took his small amount, and made enough food to feed a multitude --He will multiply whatever you give him, and ultimately what you give Him will be used to help others who are hurting.)

4. Mark 6:30-31   Jesus wants us to have time to rest.   (rest=Grk. "anapauo"
                                                                                                                to give rest, refresh,
                                                                                                                in calm and quiet
                                                                                                                and patient expectation.

Principle: It is never the Father's nature to drive us from one ministry to another with no rest. He created rest. It was His idea. He rested after Creation was accomplished.

Does this scripture indicate that Father God is concerned about the welfare and health of your physical body as well as for your soul?

_____

_____

134 | Page

5. **John 5:1-16** Jesus healed a condition of the body caused by sin, even though the man was consumed with his own inability to help himself, and made no choice of his own in that direction. (vs 6 wilt thou=Grk "thelo", to have in mind, to desire, to will
vs 14 sin=Grk. "hermartano," to err, to miss the mark, wander from God's law

thing (worse thing)= Grk."kakos", harmful, injurious, destructive, of a bad nature

Principle: Even when we cannot voice our desire for wholeness, and do not know our own hearts, consumed with our need, it is the Father's desire that we be whole in every area. Just ask Him. Tell Him your difficulty.

6. **Matthew 9:1-6** Jesus has power to heal those who have been paralyzed. (v.2 sick/palsy=Grk. "paralutikos", disabled, weak in limb
vs7 arose=Grk. "egeiro," to raise up, as from sleep, to stir)

Principle: When we cannot move ourselves, whether spiritually, in the soul, or physically, the Savior has the power to heal, awaken and restore us to wholeness.

In what way do you feel paralyzed, whether emotionally, spiritually, or physically?

_____

_____

Are you willing to do whatever Jesus tells you to do, in order to walk again?

_____

_____

(When a person feels a paralysis of soul, it is most usually a symptom of a bruised inner will. Jesus has made provision for the healing of the bruised will. He wants to help you.

The Principles and Promise of Forgiveness

"For if ye forgive men their trespasses, your heavenly Father will also forgive you. But if ye forgive not men their trespasses, neither will your Father forgive your trespasses." Matthew 6: 14-15

To forgive is to make a choice, based upon what we know is right, according to the Word of God. The decision to forgive is made with the will. The emotions of forgiveness and mercy follow as the healing process begins.

Principle: There can be no healing without the choice to forgive. It is the first step.

There are two principles to forgiveness in the Word of God.

1. The principle of Release.

--to confess the hurt, and let it go	Leviticus 16:5, and 8-10
--to give the injury to the Lord and allow Him to deal with the person in question.	Leviticus 16:10-22

To Release means that we choose to let go of the injury. We realize that Abba Father loves us, and wants to heal us of the pain of the injury. When we choose to forgive, we are making a decision to express His nature, aligning our character with His, realizing that when people are hurtful, it flows from their own pain. (See Luke 23:34) *It is the "forgive" part of "forgive and forget."*

What places of pain and injury are you now ready to choose to let the Father take into His hands, freeing you from the torment and pain of bitterness and unforgiveness? List those people and instances here.

_____

_____

_____

_____

_____

2. The principle of Remission. Leviticus 16:5, 15-16

--to sacrifice the right to hold on to the hurt; to pray the covering of the Blood of Jesus

    a. upon the hurt which was inflicted for healing and covering

    b. upon the person who inflicted the hurt for their release from bondage

When we remit, we are realizing that admitting that we have been violated. It is an acknowledgment of our right to hold on to the pain, the offense and the right to pass judgment, even silently, upon those who have hurt us. When we remit, we are letting go of those rights, and allowing Abba Father to have the last word, instead of ourselves. We are releasing the outcome and "balancing of the books," into His plan, being willing to allow Him to decide the conclusion to the story unfolding in our lives and in our relationships. When we remit, we choose to place the injustice of the offense into His hands, knowing that He will take our part, and make it right. We do this for our own health, emotional development, and spiritual growth. *It is the "forget" part of "forgive and forget."*

Are there areas where you might have made the choice to release, but have not yet made the choice to remit? List those people and instances here. Please also journal your own thoughts and feelings to the Lord as you enter into the choice to remit these offenses.

_____

_____

_____

_____

_____

There are two words used in the Greek language (New Testament) in regard to forgiveness.

<u>PRINCIPLE OF RELEASE</u> --"aphiemi" --to let go, release, to disregard, to let alone, to allow, to omit, to yield, to give up the right to, to leave alone completely

2. <u>PRINCIPLE OF REMISSION</u> --"aphesis" --to release from bondage, to pardon, to remove the penalty, to deliver

What the New Testament Teaches About Forgiveness

(Note: Forgiveness and Healing are separate processes in the soul, and must be pursued individually. A refusal to forgive someone who has wounded us will keep us from moving forward in the healing process; Reciprocally, an attitude of denial and refusal to face woundings, bruises and fear, will stop the process of forgiveness. Without both of these elements working together in the life of the disciple, there can be no forward movement or growth.

Forgiveness is:

1. It is an attitude of heart, which is not easily provoked to anger or revenge. If someone is harsh or demanding, we are to have a forgiving nature beforehand.	I Corinthians 13:4-7 Matthew 5:40 ("Let have" = "aphiemi")

(Note: Forgiveness flows from the source of unconditional Love." If you have an inability to love someone, pray Romans 5:5 over your own heart. Realize that Abba Father will send the Spirit to shed His love abroad into your heart.)

2. It means to completely forgive and forget the incident. To leave it behind entirely.	Matthew 4:20-22 ("left" = "aphiemi") Luke 5:11 ("forsook all" = "aphiemi")
3. To the degree we forgive, we will be forgiven.	Matthew 6:12-15 ("forgive"="aphiemi") Mark 11:25 Luke 11:4 John 20:23
4. We are to forgive an unlimited number of times within the same day for the same offense, from the heart.	Matthew 18: 21-35
5. The degree of our love for the Lord is dependent upon the degree of forgiveness we ask. (How deep is the level of consecration in your heart?)	Luke 7:47-48
6. If someone trespasses (violate private property) against us, Jesus taught that we should let them know we were hurt by their actions. If they are sorry, we cannot hold on to the hurt, we must let it go and choose to forgive them. We are not to "attach strings" to our forgiveness.	Luke 17:3-4
7. The Father wants us to ask for forgiveness when we have evil thoughts.	Acts 8:22
8. When we are forgiven, we are blessed.	Romans 4:7
9. In order to be forgiven, we must confess our sin. Then, the Father can cleanse us completely.	I John 1:9
10. We are to follow Christ's example, and forgive things done against us in ignorance.	Luke 23:34

A Scripture-Based Prayer
To Help in Releasing Forgiveness

(this prayer is most effective when prayed in agreement with someone Trustworthy – in community and safety – for healing and wholeness)

Father God, thank you for your love for me. I know that you love me unconditionally.

I choose to walk in Your ways.

Thank you for the gift of your Son, Who died so that I might live forever.

Father, I choose to forgive everyone who has knowingly or even unknowingly inflicted hurts and bruises upon my life.

I choose to be a generous and forgiving person.

With my will, I will forgive, and I trust You to fill my heart
with your love and the feelings of forgiveness in the days to come.

Father, I choose to release and relinquish all of my rights
to hold on to these hurts and bruises. I choose to confess
them to you, and allow you to be the vindicator and Healer of my Heart.

For my own health, I let go of (name the person and the instance by name)
I let go of my right to be hurt, or to hold onto offense.

I give it to You, to vindicate me, and bring right out of the situation.

I allow you to open my heart. Please help me to grieve my losses well.

Thank you for your peace.

In Jesus' name, Amen.

Notes Regarding Bondages

A bondage is an action or practice, thought or habit pattern, which a person cannot seem to discipline themselves to bring to an end. Even when they think they have some degree of victory over the problem, a "hunger pang" for a particular experience of sin will act as a handle upon their soul, which Satan uses to pull them back into defeat and condemnation. This in itself is an evidence of demonic influence.

Bondages show themselves in addictions, generational tendencies, and in outright selfish choices.

Things which bind the soul (giving the devil a legal right to hold the person in a cycle of bondage:

1. Promises made, or vows	Deuteronomy 23:21-22 Numbers 30:9
2. Lies which have been told	John 8:32
3. The rejection of abstinence from sexual immorality is actually a rejection of God.	I Thessalonians 4:1-8
4. Anxiety is in the heart because of sin in the heart. (There must a recognition of the need for deliverance.)	Psalm 38:17-22
5. To take counsel other than God's to heart before His counsel is rebellion. a. procrastination is rebellion	Isaiah 30: 1

New Horizons!! Lessons for Liberty

Part Three –

"Jesus is Our Joshua"

The Choice

Joshua stood on the crest of the hill and looked over the camp of his people. It had been a long tour of duty. And the promise! The promise was just about to be fulfilled!! His heart beat a little faster, and his energy returned.

He looked over at Caleb. Caleb smiled,

"I know we can do this! To think God gave it to *us!"* was **all** Caleb said. It was all he had said for the last six miles of the journey.

'1 know," Joshua patted his friend on the shoulder. "1 can't wait to share the things we have seen with the people; to think that God has given us --us! -- such a miraculous gift! Just imagine it! We will have our own homes, and even our own wells..."

Excited, Caleb nodded and interrupted him. "And no one will whip us in the field. We can work at the things we want to work at… We will be able to raise our children in peace."

"It will be wonderful."

"Lets go on down to the camp."

Full of anticipation, Joshua and Caleb proceeded down the hill, just a little ahead of the others.

They had been two of twelve; twelve spies sent into the land of Canaan to look it over, and assess what military action should be taken next. How should Israel proceed?

God had promised the land, but what was the next step?

The other ten men who had traveled with them were also arriving at the campfires.

Moses left the circle of elders at the fire first. He ran to greet Joshua, embracing him with the heartfelt warmth of a father. It was Moses who had nicknamed him "Joshua", from his name "Hoshea;" it was Moses who had taught him the ways of God.

Joshua could still remember the first time he had followed Moses to the tabernacle and seen the cloud of the Presence.

"It's good to have you back. We're anxious to hear your report. How was the land?" Moses hugged Caleb as well. "Is it all we had hoped it would be?"

"It's a beautiful land! Look! There are the grapes we brought back!" Caleb pointed to two men behind him who were carrying single cluster of gigantic grapes hanging from a pole hoisted on their shoulders. It almost touched the ground.

Caleb waved his arm to a third who was carrying a huge basket on his head. "And the honeycomb!! Talk about a sweet life!"

"That is just one bunch of grapes?" A little girl asked Joshua. A crowd had joined the spies as they walked. The people were gathering into a procession. Everyone wanted to see and hear what the spies had discovered.

Joshua scooped her up in his arms. "Yes, sweetheart; and that's just *one* bunch. You should see the land the Lord has given us. It is massive."

They had all arrived at the campfire now. The elders rose up to those returning from their own tribe. Joshua and Caleb's families were there as well, to extend a welcome.

Joshua put the little girl down and greeted his wife. It was so good to be home. He lifted his arms and spoke to the gathering.

"The land the Lord has given us is truly a land of promise! It is a great place, and a place where we will be free!"

A voice spoke from the back of the crowd.

"We're free now, Joshua."

"But this is a greater degree of freedom than you have ever known; or I; or any of us."

"Is it as good as Egypt?" It was another voice.

A woman spoke up. "Anything is better than this desert!"

Caleb answered. "It's much better. Think of it. Owning your own home, and your own land, and no one beating you down in the field."

"Yeah, but did you tell them about the giants?" Shaphat, from the tribe of Simeon, had just a hint of anger in his voice.

"Giants? What *giants*?"

"And what about the cities?" Gaddiel, another of the spies, looked around at the people as he spoke. "You should see this place. The giants are *so* big --I couldn't believe it. The size of the grapes should be an indication as to the size of the people we will be fighting. Think about it. Doesn't that tell you what we are up against?"

"No one knows what we are up against any more than I do, Gaddiel." Joshua raised his voice to reach to the back of the congregation. "Caleb and I saw the same things you saw." He climbed to stand up on a rock as he spoke. He wanted to be able to see the back row of the gathered crowd of Israelites. He continued to speak.

"But it is a matter of choice. Will we believe what God has spoken? Will we go into the land and take it, because He has promised to give it to us?

"What will we believe?"

The Problem of the Bruised Will

*"A bruised reed shall he not break,
a smoking flax shall he not quench,
til He send forth judgment unto victory."* Matthew 12:20

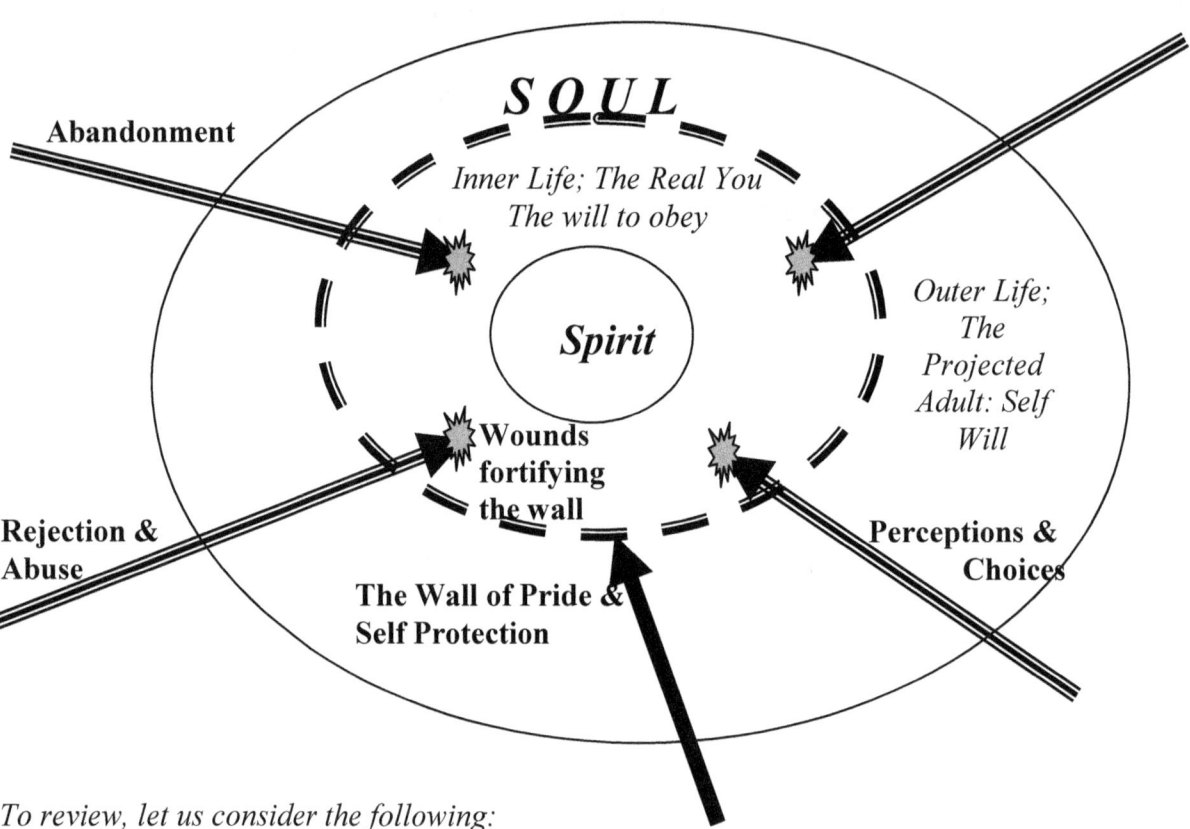

To review, let us consider the following:

Problem: The soul of man carries the consequences of the willful choice made in Eden. The ingesting of the fruit allowed the poison of Satan's disposition to permeate every area of the personality.

The natural tendencies of the human soul changed from likeness of Father God (in His image), to those of Satan himself. Adam and Eve became ruled by their inner will, rather than led by the spirit, and their spirits within them died. Because of their choice to sin, every human being born on the planet since Eden, must experience a re-birth of spirit in order to enter into God's plan and purpose.

Because Satan has targeted every person's life on the planet for destruction, the inner will is bruised and unable to function as it was created to function. Without spiritual re-birth, there can be no stability or strength to overcome weaknesses within the life. The person is driven by their needs, feelings, and circumstances, rather than by faith in the Son of God, and the Word of God.

Solution:

The soul must be transformed by the same explosive resurrection power, which regenerated the spirit of man. An intentional choice must be made in every area of the soul, turning the heart toward the likeness of Father God. Each area of the mind, the will, and the emotions must be intentionally surrendered to the Will and Plan of God. We must realize that it is Satan's desire that we repeat the process of Eden's fall on a daily basis, ignoring our weaknesses, and hiding our sin from the all-seeing eyes of Father God.

We intentionally and willfully choose to align our belief systems with what the Word of God says – and *only* what the Word of God says, by making application of Abba Father's truth to our lives. We cannot lean on experiences or traditions.

Observation: Eve's sin came through deception. She actually believed that she was doing the right thing --that somehow her actions were bring her closer to God. Adam's sin was willful and deliberate. He knew and remembered exactly what Father God had said, but chose to follow his wife's leading, and bought the lies of rebellion.

 (See I Timothy 2:14, I Corinthians 15:22, and Romans 10:12)

Both types of sin bring death. One is not less destructive than the other.

Principle:

Confession brings Covering (I John 1:9, Genesis 3:8-12 and 21)

> *Note: Because of wounds and bruises within the soul, the inner will is bruised.*
> *Decisions made are difficult to keep due to the overwhelming of the soul by*
> *fear, shame, guilt, and many other emotions. Only the Word of God, and the*
> *Spirit of God can bring healing and a fortification of the will to choose God's Way.*

Becoming Free From Self-Will

Definition: Stubborn resistance to the hand of God; an apathy toward personal spiritual growth; (Blaming others for one's own lack of growth.) The setting of a personal goal, with the expectation and sense of entitlement to God's Blessing; rather than seeking of God's goal and purpose prior to setting the goal; the self-sufficiency which handles difficulties in its own strength, without seeking God first for the answers. Self-will is the control of your own environment. It is rule and structure oriented. It is also called a hardness of heart.

Principle: The more self-will is in control of the life, the weaker the believer will find him or herself in being able to follow through with decisions to obey the Word of God. The desire will be present, without the strength. *"No man can serve two masters." (Matthew 6:24)*

Problem: The heart has become weak in its ability to believe truth, and accept that truth as the final authority for living. Personal perceptions, emotions, and imprinted thought processes rule the life. The conscience has become weak in its ability to distinguish right from wrong. The will cannot decide to obey and hold to any positive decision for growth and change. The will is bruised and has become passive.

It is important that a person understand that when we don't choose the Lord's way and follow it intentionally and aggressively, we have chosen to remain influenced by the enemy and be filled with self-will.

Solution: The heart, the conscience and the will must be strengthened in progressive steps, to support and make permanent the healing process. Passivity must be turned into hard line obedience by the application of the Word of God.

What is Self-Will?

It is the sin of stubbornness.	
It is forbidden	II Chronicles 30:8
It proceeds from unbelief	II Kings 17:14
(lack of trust that God can do what He says He will do)	
It is pride	Nehemiah 9:16 and 29
It doesn't listen to God	Proverbs 1:24
It doesn't listen to his messengers	I Samuel 8:19
	Jeremiah 44:16
	Zechariah 7:11
It refuses to receive correction	Deuteronomy 21:18
It causes a person's spiritual growth to regress	Jeremiah 7:24
In God's eyes, it is idolatry and insubordination	I Samuel 15:19-23

Looking at the previous page, make a worksheet for your own benefit, outlining your understanding to this point of how your life has operated in self-will.

In what areas of your life have you taken charge, so that you would not cease to function as a normal person?

_____

_____

Are there areas of your heart in which you find it difficult to trust other people? Why? List those areas here.

_____

_____

In what ways do you feel you have had to become a survivor just to continue living?

_____

_____

What wounds and difficulties are now coming to mind, which have inhibited your growth, and caused the fear of pain to be the motivation for your life?

_____

_____

Write out a short prayer of consecration and trust here, naming those who have hurt you, and releasing forgiveness.

_____

_____

_____

_____

The Heart of Man

"Wait on the Lord; be of good courage, and He shall strengthen thine heart: Wait, I say on the Lord." Psalm 27: 14

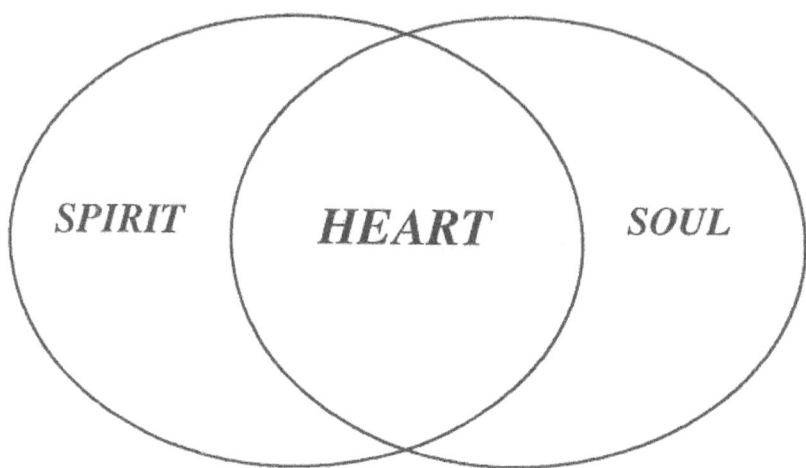

Description: The heart is referred to many times in the Scriptures. It is described in both a good and bad sense. It has spiritual qualities, as well as those of the soul.

Therefore, the heart of man is the place within him, where the two areas of soul and spirit are combined. It is the emotional and convictional part of his being. It involves parts of his will as well as his emotions. For this reason, many times a person will experience an inner battle between what they know they should do (spirit led), and what they feel they want to do (soul-led).

In order for the life of a man or woman to become transformed, it must be turned (or inclined) toward the Lord.

The Bruised Will and the Heart of Man

Biblical definition of the word "Heart" –
The inner part, inclination, resolution and determination.
The seat of man's appetites and emotions.

1. Imaginations and thoughts come from the heart.   Proverbs 12:20

When a person suffers from a bruised will, the imaginations and thoughts of the heart continually confront and question the knowledge and authority of the Word of God. The broken self-image of a person gives way to worry, and thoughts of terrible occurrences to oneself, one's family and loved ones. Also brought to the mind are "images" (imaginations) of a person's life goals. These imaginations must be constantly warred against within. Write out II Corinthians 10:5 here.

_____

_____

_____

2. The heart is the part of man inclined to trust   Judges 9:3
someone else, or to be part of a cause.

In II Samuel, chapters 14 and 15, the account is given of David's son, Absalom, and how he stole the loyalty of the hearts of the people of Israel away from the king. God created us to be a part of something bigger than ourselves. We are designed to fit into His plan for our lives, rather than fabricate our own plan and ask His blessing. Psalm 28:7 shows us two results of seeking to be a part of God's cause, rather than simply trying to operate on our own. Write Psalm 28:7 here.

_____

_____

_____

3. The heart can be unified or divided in its allegiances.   Psalm 12:2
   Psalm 119:1,2 & 10

In I Chronicles 12:23-38, the account is given of who was supported the crowning of King David, when he was made king over the nation of Israel. The term "perfect heart" is used to describe these men in verse 38. The Hebrew word "shalem" has been translated "perfect" in this Scripture, meaning "complete, whole or at peace". How are these same men described in I Chronicles 12:33?

   a. Able to keep _____ . (This describes someone who is able to work well with authority figures.

   b. Not of _____ heart. What does James 1:5-8 say in regard to a person with this problem? What effect does this condition have on all the components of his or her life?

   _____

   _____

4. The heart is the part of man that responds to God   Psalm 27:8

In Isaiah 29:13, Father God speaks to the nation of Israel, illustrating the condition of their heart as a nation. In what way does the prophet describe the condition of Israel's divided heart?

   _____

   _____

What is a person who operates with a divided heart actually preparing for themselves as a future consequence?

Job 36:13 _____

What observation is made regarding those who serve God with an undivided heart?

Psalm 119:2 _____

Do you want to be blessed? _____

Are there any areas of your heart where you feel your ability to choose well might be divided? Write them here. Then write out a prayer for understanding as to the cause of that division. Also, ask for Father God's healing touch.

_____

_____

5. The heart can become calloused, dull of hearing, and blind to the things of God.

In Matthew 13:15, Jesus is describing the hearts of the Pharisees, and he uses the Greek word "pachuno", which is translated in the King James Version of the Bible as "waxed gross". The heart which has "waxed gross" has done so over a period of time, through a gradual process of hardening. It is like the development of a callous upon the soul, one layer at a time. Many times, it is indicative of a person who has leaned on formulas and patterns to mold their spiritual life, rather than a personally intimate relationship with Father God and His Son, Jesus. A person with this condition of heart finds it difficult to understand spiritual truths, and finds it difficult to feel close to Father God, or to sense His Spirit. A person in this condition is led, many times, by the opinions of his/her peers, and the general consensus of his society, rather than the Word of God. What counsel does Christ Himself give to a church in this condition in Revelation 3:18? Write that counsel here. (Laos = people/ Dicea = rulership --Laodicea= "a place where the people rule")

_____

_____

Read II Corinthians 3:12-18.

Are there any areas of your life you sense might be "veiled" from receiving the fullness of the touch of the Spirit of God? Write out a prayer for healing and deliverance here.

_____

_____

7. Man cannot consider the miracles of God when he has a hard heart.

In Mark 6:52, why didn't Jesus' disciples expect a miracle? _____

What account of their hearts is given in Mark 16:14? _____

8. The word of faith is stored (through memorization) in the heart.

What is its purpose, according to Psalm 119:18? _____

How is faith instilled within the heart? Write out Romans 10:17 here.

_____

_____

9. The heart chooses to believe.   Romans 10:9-10

   Notice that what we say (our confession) contributes much to salvation.

   a. An unbelieving heart is called an evil heart.   Hebrews 3:12
   b. The heart faints (becomes numb or weak)   Genesis 45:26
   because of unbelief. (example: Jacob)

Because belief is a choice, many times, when we choose to believe what Father God has promised, it goes against what we feel. Therefore, in order to bring our heart into a place of liberty, it is important that we actively and forcibly choose (sometimes on a daily basis) that we will believe and adhere to what the Word of God says.

Is there anything that you can think of, right now, which you need to choose to believe God to take care of in your own life?

_____

_____

_____

10. The layers upon the heart can be pierced, or circumcised, so that the true feelings and attitudes of a person's life become evident. This is what makes a person truly converted and changed. This process is powered by the Word of God.

The inner will, that part of man existing behind the wall of Pride, is what receives conviction to change. What two responses to conviction are shown in the Scriptures below?

Acts 2:37 _____

Acts 7:54 _____

What actions does the Word of God perform in our hearts? See Hebrews 4:12

    a. dividing _____ and _____

(helping us understand what is our own emotions, and what He is speaking to our inner spirit.)

    b. discerner (helping us to see clearly) the _____ and

_____ of the _____ .

11. Whatever fills the heart will come out of the mouth.   Matthew 12:34-35

What words do you find yourself saying in regard to your own life, and regretting later? (It is a good idea to keep track of your confession -God does. See Proverbs 18:21 What you hear coming out of your own mouth, can be a good indication of what is hidden within your heart).

_____

What kind of words and heart attitude does Psalm 39:3 describe? _____

12. The heart of Father God toward us is the same, no matter the condition of our heart. (See I John 3:20). He desires and is capable of accomplishing the following within us.

The Father can prepare the heart. What promise is made to us in Psalm 10:17?

_____

Write out Psalm 119:32 here.

_____

_____

b. The Father can replace the heart, and empower a person to be obedient to His will and plan. What observation is made about Saul's change of heart in I Samuel 10:9?

_____

c. The heart receives mercy from the Father when its allegiance to Him is unified. His Presence rests there, and His promises (covenants) are honored. Read Solomon's words in II Chronicles 6:14 --Write a prayer for His mercy here.

_____

_____

d. It is Father God who softens the heart	Job 23:16
e. It is Father God who puts gladness into the heart of man.	Psalm 4:7
f. The heart is strengthened by the grace of God.	Hebrews 13:9
g. It is Father God who speaks commission (purpose and direction for life) into the heart of man.	II Chronicles 7:11 II Chronicles 9:23 Ezra 7:27
h. The heart which is set upon the Father, is glad, and the flesh rests in hope.	Psalm 16:9

Are there areas of relational ministry to the heart, which you see listed above, and cannot seem to take hold of for your own life? List them here.

_____

_____

What do the scriptures describe your own heart, listed above, show to be the pathway to freedom for your heart to experience relational understanding of the love of the Father for you?

_____

The Conscience of Man

*"How much more shall the blood of Christ, who through the eternal
Spirit offered himself without spot to God,
purge your conscience from dead works to serve the living God?"* Hebrews 9: 14

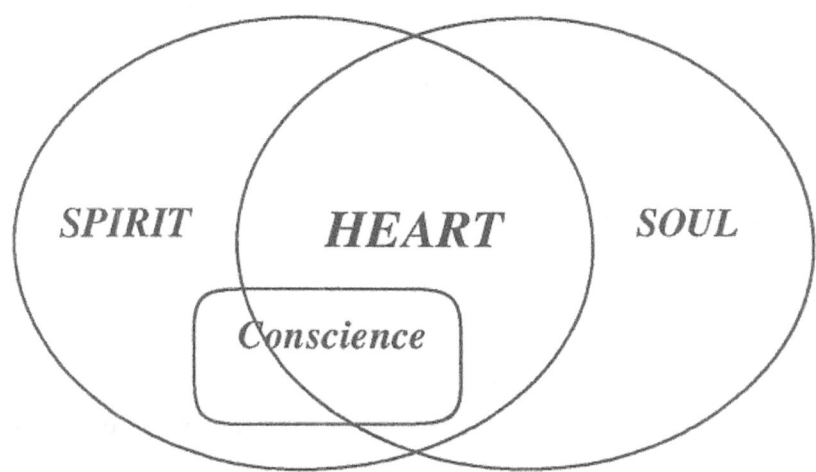

Description: The conscious part of a man or woman, which is able to distinguish between right and wrong, in the moral sense. The part which urges man to make the right choice. In the heart and spirit of the believer, the conscience is the deep inner sense of the leading of the Spirit of God.

(Greek -"suneidesis", the consciousness, the ability to distinguish)

In the day-to-day walk of the Christian Life, we are constantly learning to distinguish between the voice of our own conscience, and the Voice of the Holy Spirit. This is called the purging process. (Hebrews 9:14)

The Bruised Will and the Human Conscience

*"How much more shall the blood of Christ, who through
the eternal Spirit offered himself without spot to God,
purge your conscience from dead works to serve the living God?" Hebrews 9: 14*

1. What are the Scriptural operations of the human conscience?

    a. The conscience tells us when we are telling the truth.   Romans 9:1

    b. We are convicted by the conscience when we have sin in our hearts.   John 8:9

    c. The conscience bears witness (agrees) with the work of God's Law.   Romans 2:15

Which of the above listed acts of the human conscience do you currently see as active in your own life? (circle one)

All   A   B   C   a combination   none listed

2. What are the evidences of a healthy conscience? (A healthy conscience operates to its **full** potential of what Father God created.)

    a. The mystery of faith must be held on to by the conscience.   I Timothy 3:9

    b. The testimony of a good conscience is simplicity and godly sincerity, which does not depend on fleshly wisdom (man's opinions), but on the Grace of God.   II Corinthians 1:12

    c. The testimony of a good conscience evidences itself in a person's willingness to endure grief and suffer wrongfully for the sake of what is believed to be true.   I Peter 2:19 / I Peter 3:16

In what areas of your life do you now see the evidence of a good conscience?

_____

_____

d. In I Timothy 1:5, we are told what things accompany a good conscience. Write them here.

1. _____ 2. _____

3. What damages the conscience?

      a. hypocrisy   I Timothy 4:2

(the word "hypocrite" comes from the concept of wearing masks to communicate a character's nature. Hypocrisy is the act of wearing a mask to hide the real person. This keeps a person from receiving all Jesus has for them --the real person inside the heart.)

Can you think of any way in which you have allowed your true identity to be masked, weakening the ability of your conscience? Write out a prayer of confession here.

_____

_____

      b. unbelief   Titus 1:15

      c. defilement (touching things that are unclean --thoughts, habits, etc.   Titus 1:15

      d. A weak conscience can be defiled when we know something is wrong, and do it anyway.   I Corinthians 8:7-12

      e. Neglecting to develop and nurture the conscience with the applied Word of God can cause a person to become shipwrecked in their faith.   I Timothy 1:9

(Note: The conscience can be cleansed by the sprinkling of the Blood of Jesus. Just pray and ask Jesus to wash your conscience in His Blood, cleansing it and calling it to life. Then, set a daily time to read the Word of God, allowing your inner will to be strengthened, and your conscience to grow its ability to make you aware of right and wrong.)

Write down here what daily time you will commit to set aside for this growth to take place.

_____

f. A man with a weak conscience is caused to stumble (find fault and sin) by another man's careless disregard and sin.   I Corinthians 8: 12

Are there any areas in your life in which you have made a decision to "just do it anyway -- I'm an adult, I can", or said or thought, "It's my life; I can do what I want to"? If you have made these decisions without regard to those brothers and sisters in the Lord who might be weaker or less mature, it is possible that you have caused a brother or sister to sin by your example and lack of witness. Write the areas the Holy Spirit is bringing to mind here.

_____

_____

4. What strengthens the conscience?

       a. Write out I Peter 3:21 here.

_____

_____

       b. When we are obedient to God's delegated authorities (family, church, employment and government), that obedience confirms, strengthens and protects our conscience. Read Romans 13:1-5. Then write out a list of God's delegated authorities in your own life.

_____

_____

_____

How Do I Strengthen My Heart and Conscience to Choose Abba's Way? How Do I Stop Operating in Passivity?

The heart and conscience both operate with influence from the human will.
When a person's will has been bruised, the heart and mind become passive, and unable to make decisions for lasting change. Mental patterns will be easily influenced by sudden flashes of thought, and an inability to maintain any kind of follow-through within the life takes hold.
A person becomes the victim of their own emotions, memories, and circumstances.
In strengthening the heart and conscience, there are several misconceptions which will usually begin to surface, inhibiting inhibit spiritual growth. These mindsets should be intentionally addressed for change, in order for the heart and conscience to be enabled to consistently
hear the voice of the Holy Spirit.

1. Misconception #1 - I must give up my own will.

Realize that the human will cannot be set aside in order for a person to live the Christian life. We live the Christian life, choosing to be obedient of our own accord. We do not give up our thinking processes in the Christian life, nor does Abba Father desire us to become dormant inside so that Christ can use us.

The Right Choice: To submit myself to God in all circumstances. To choose to be relational in my spiritual life, and not just adhere to a structure of obedience, obeying my Father because I desire to please Him, not because it is what the rules dictate.

What commitment do you need to make in this regard? Write it out here.

_____

2. Misconception #2 -- I can only be spiritually strong when I am weak.

We do not make a decision to be weak so that Christ can be strong through us. We ask for His strength when we have difficulty obeying, and when we are overcome by our own weaknesses.

The Right Choice: To use all of my being to obey the Word of God, applying myself in every area. When I have difficulty, I will ask for His strength to under-gird me in my weakness. I will be honest with myself, God and other people about my negative emotions. I cannot be a perfect person, but I can allow the Perfection of Jesus to be seen through me, even when I am weak, and unable to follow through on my own.

What change in your thought patterns must take place, in order for this understanding to be put in action? Why?

_____

_____

3. Misconception #3 --All of my circumstances are God's will for my life.

Realize that every circumstance *is* not God's will for your *life,* (although Romans 8:28 teaches us that He will work all things together for good --even those negative situations can have a positive outcome when we give them over to His hand.) Every situation is not His choice for us. Father God is not a destructive force. This misunderstanding causes double-mindedness and unstable faith. He will give us the discernment to know when to fight against the enemy. And then we *must* choose to fight.

The Right Choice: To not accept every situation which comes upon my life without prayer and discernment. I will choose to pray and do battle against what seeks to destroy my spiritual life, without passive acceptance.

What changes have to take place in your thinking in order for you to become a warrior in regard to your own spiritual life? Journal your commitment to those changes here.

_____

_____

4. Misconception #4 --God is like fate. What happens is His Will. I will walk into His will without effort.

Each person has a destiny and calling upon their life. Those places of development do not just happen. Seek the Father, to find out what His will is for your life. Nothing will strengthen your will more than having it in line with God's will. (This will begin small – not with larger life-changing decisions) Find out what basic things are His will for you. Now: where you are.

The Right Choice: I will seek to become all that God wants me to be. I will seek to make my life choices in line with His direction for my life.

What understanding do you currently have of God's will and direction for your life?

_____

_____

5. Misconception #5 --God wants me to be happy. When I am happy, I am in His will.

Things and *circumstances* are not what determine God's will. Prosperity does not necessarily indicate His blessing. Health and wellness of soul and spirit are what indicate His will and blessing. Many times, we are distracted by those things we want, rather than directed into the Presence of Father God for healing and fulfillment. Learn to tell yourself "no." Not everything our inner self wants is necessary for spiritual health. Find out what the Word of God says is necessary, and do *it*. Memorize the Word to protect your will and heart from *sinning against* God.

The Right Choice: I will deny myself those things which feed my carnal appetites. I will memorize the Word of God to strengthen myself.

In what areas of your life do you find that your will currently responding in a passive manner? Where do you find it difficult to hold to a decision for personal change?

___

___

6. Misconception #6 - I can relax and trust those who I know to be spiritual around me to direct my life. I can follow their understanding for my life. Submission means I can have no feelings, desires or direction of my own.

Realize the only way to strengthen the passive will is by making decisions. Stop asking other people what they think *you* should do, without making your own decisions. If you are unsure about a decision, it is all right to seek counsel, or to ask someone you respect to give you input regarding a decision you are in the process of making, before you take action. But try to make your own decisions first. Purpose to obey God. Then do your best. The Father knows the condition of your will. When you fail, ask *for forgiveness and try again. The Father has sent the Holy Spirit to teach you* and to guide *you* into all truth. Remember to keep yourself in balance, however, and don't negate the counsel of the spiritual leadership the Father has placed in your life (your pastor, and godly church leadership).

The Right Choice: To seek to hear the voice of God for myself, and not lean totally upon the second-hand instruction others give me for my life. I set my will to trust God.

In what areas of your life do you realize you have been operating with a passive heart and conscience? How have you stopped making decisions?

___

How have you allowed your heart to become shut off? Are there areas of your life in which you feel numb, and unable to function in a relational manner?

_____

_____

Write out a prayer, asking for Abba Father God's help in engaging your heart again.

_____

_____

_____

_____

Note:

*Your will must be strengthened
in order to maintain freedom in any area of your life.*

You are the one doing the warfare!!

How To Strengthen Your Will
To Choose Abba Father's Way

The following are suggestions for you to follow when you find your will is weak and somewhat unwilling to obey the Spirit of the Lord, or authority figures He has placed in your life. Any one of these suggestions will help to strengthen your will. As you find yourself becoming stronger in obedience, it is a good idea to add more steps, until all have been completed.

The **minimum** time spent on each of these steps should be 30 days. Do not try to rush through these steps. Accomplishment does not bring immediate healing. Growth always takes a little time.

~~~~~~~~~~

1. Choose and commit to pray in the Spirit for 1 hour a day. (Do not plan to do this all at once. Pray in 12 increments of 5 minutes, or 6 increments of 10 minutes at regular times each day.) It works well to set a timer, so that you do not short yourself on the edifying benefit of prayer.

2. Choose and commit to read the Word of God. Read 5-15 verses **out loud** to yourself on a daily basis. Read the same portion of scripture 3 times through. Here are some recommended sections, which will shine the Father's light on your will.

Ephesians 2: 1-10	Ephesians 4:30-32	Colossians 3:1-10
John 14:23-30	Colossians 3:5-11	Revelation 3:14-22
II Corinthians 3:1-18	Luke 6:46-48	Ephesians 4:14-22
Ephesians 5:1-12	Colossians 2:6-10	Colossians 1:9-14
I Thessalonians 5:8-23	II Corinthians 4:1-7	John 15:1-11

3. Choose and commit to memorizing the Word of God, with references. Quote the scriptures you have memorized to those who are walking your through the process of strengthening your will. Here are some suggested verses:

John 4:34   John 6:38   Matthew 26:41   Matthew 7:13-14

4. Choose and commit to worship the Father for a specific amount of undistracted, private time - just you and God. Set 3 minutes as a beginning place. This should be stretched into a fifteen minute segment as your will progresses in obedience. If need be, set a timer to help you. Sing worship songs, and focus on the Father's love for you.

5. Choose and commit to do a word study from the Word of God on Obedience.

6. Choose and commit to fast two meals in one day, and read the Word instead of eating. Read Psalm 23 through Psalm 34 out loud to yourself each time you do so. This should be done once a month to begin with, and then progressively brought into a weekly practice.

7. On a piece of paper, make two columns. Label the columns, "Things which strengthen my will to obey", and "Things which weaken my will to obey." Look up the following scriptures and fill in the categories you find.

I Peter 3:21	I Timothy 4:2	Titus 1:5
I Timothy 1:9	Romans 13:5	Romans 6:16
Romans 8:7	Galatians 3:1	Matthew 7:21
I Corinthians 8:12	Romans 2:15	James 3:18
Romans 2:6-10	Proverbs 6:12-15	Joshua 24:24
Acts 5:32	Galatians 5:7	Matthew 7:24-27
Proverbs 1:28-31	Matthew 24:12	Titus 3:1
Hebrews 13:17	Hebrews 12:9	Nehemiah 9:17
Romans 2:8	John 14:15	I Chronicles 12:33

8. Rewrite the following scriptures, and substitute personal and impersonal pronouns with your own first name, and "his/him or hers/her", etc. Then commit yourself to memorize each one.

Romans 8:15	Deuteronomy 31:8	Isaiah 43:1-3
Isaiah 41:10	Psalm 23	Philippians 1:6
II Thessalonians 3:3	Isaiah 54:14,15, and 17	I John 4:4
Luke 10:19	II Timothy 4:18	Isaiah 42:16
Lamentations 3:22	Isaiah 59:11	Ezekiel 34:16
Jeremiah 29:11	Hebrews 13:5	Psalm 120:7
I Corinthians 10:13	I Corinthians 1:5	Acts 2:39

9. Keep a journal of the scriptures and truths which have become real to your own heart. When pain comes close to the surface these things will encourage your heart and help you.

10. When your emotions rise up, and try to control your actions and responses, by using painful memories and experiences, take the time to write them down. Then, find an accountability friend (someone who you can trust to keep things confidential and whose love you are secure with), to pray through each instance with. It is also a good idea to take communion, and apply the blood of Jesus specifically to each area in question.

"Say What?"

Joshua's wife stood in the middle of the crowd. She could hear the voices of her family and neighbors around her.

"Giants? How big is a giant?"

"I bet we look like grasshoppers next to them. How can you fight something that big? They will destroy us!"

"Sure, the fruit looks great. But it's got to be harder than just walking in and building a house. Somebody already owns that land. You know?"

"Is Moses sure this is where God wants us to go?"

"Yeah, I know what you mean. Maybe he's just doing this because he won't ever be Pharaoh. Maybe it's his own idea."

"What if we should have never left Egypt? Maybe that's why things are the way they are."

The tension was mounting, and the murmurs were getting louder.

Then Moses spoke.

"Tell us about the land," he said.

"What did you see?"

One by one, the spies gave their reports. They told the people of all they had seen. Yes, it was a land, green and lush, full of brooks and streams. It had plenty of wildlife, and vegetation. The land was ready to be farmed. It was beautiful.

                              Just as God had said.

They told of the cities in the land; of Jericho, with walls so thick that people lived inside them. They told of giants. They told of giant grapevines and clusters of grapes. They told it all.

Listening carefully, Joshua's wife noticed something. Ten of the spies gave more than a report of what they had seen. They also shared their fear of the land and their personal inner struggle to believe. These ten could not see how the God who had delivered them from Egypt could conquer the difficulties they faced. They mixed their report with the intimidation they felt, and gave a negative report.

An *evil* report.

Standing with his wife, Joshua watched the response of the people as these reports were given. He and Caleb had chosen to wait until the last to share. They wanted the last thing the people heard to be words of faith.

Faith in God's ability to keep His promise.

But it did not matter. When Joshua's turn came, the people seemed to be deaf.

They were so accustomed to slavery that it was easier for them to give up than to fight their way through. They began to moan and complain. They wailed at Moses.

They accused him.

"Why did you bring us out into this wilderness to die?"

"We were better off in Egypt!"

Joshua could not believe his ears.

Never mind the Blood of the Lamb had redeemed them from slavery on Passover.
Never mind that they had been delivered from destruction through
the crossing of the Red Sea.
Forget that Pharaoh and all his army could never touch them again.

Never mind that the Father had sent manna --angels" bread --to feed them each morning!
Never mind He had given them water from a rock, and meat when they asked for it.

Sure. They had been better off in Egypt.

Like a straw house would be better off in a hurricane.

What was wrong with these people??

He shouted above the clamor. The crowd quieted down; but only temporarily.

"Wait! Don't believe these bad reports! Would God promise you something He wouldn't deliver? Has He ever failed to keep His word to you? What has He promised that He has not done?

"We can take this land. Yes, it will be a fight. But we have God on our side. He will not fail us! Choose His promise. Choose His way!!"

Caleb and his family cheered. Joshua's family cheered. Moses cheered.

But the rest of the congregation was silent.

    And in their silence, they made their choice.

In not taking intentional action,
    In refusing to choose to obey,
        By giving consideration to everyone's opinions instead of following the Commands of the Father ……….   They chose.
        By choosing to stand still, they chose to disobey:
            To remain free from Egypt's slavery, but live in the wilderness.   To exist and subsist, just wandering from place to place --without   purpose or plan.
Without a vision;

    A people without a country.

Abba Father, their God and Creator waited –
    holding victory in one hand, and milk and honey in the other.

If only they would choose.

    And Joshua wondered,
        When would the sons of Adam stop choosing death instead of life?

> **Please listen to the ninth CD, utilizing your notebook, for Session Nine**
>
> **"The Power of the Speaking Blood"**
> **before you move ahead**

Notes:

Satan's Bruise of Rejection

*There is a progression to bruising the soul of man.
Satan begins with the infliction of Rejection upon the life in one area or another.
He will use family, peers, circumstances, physical appearances, thought patterns and perceptions as his weapons.*

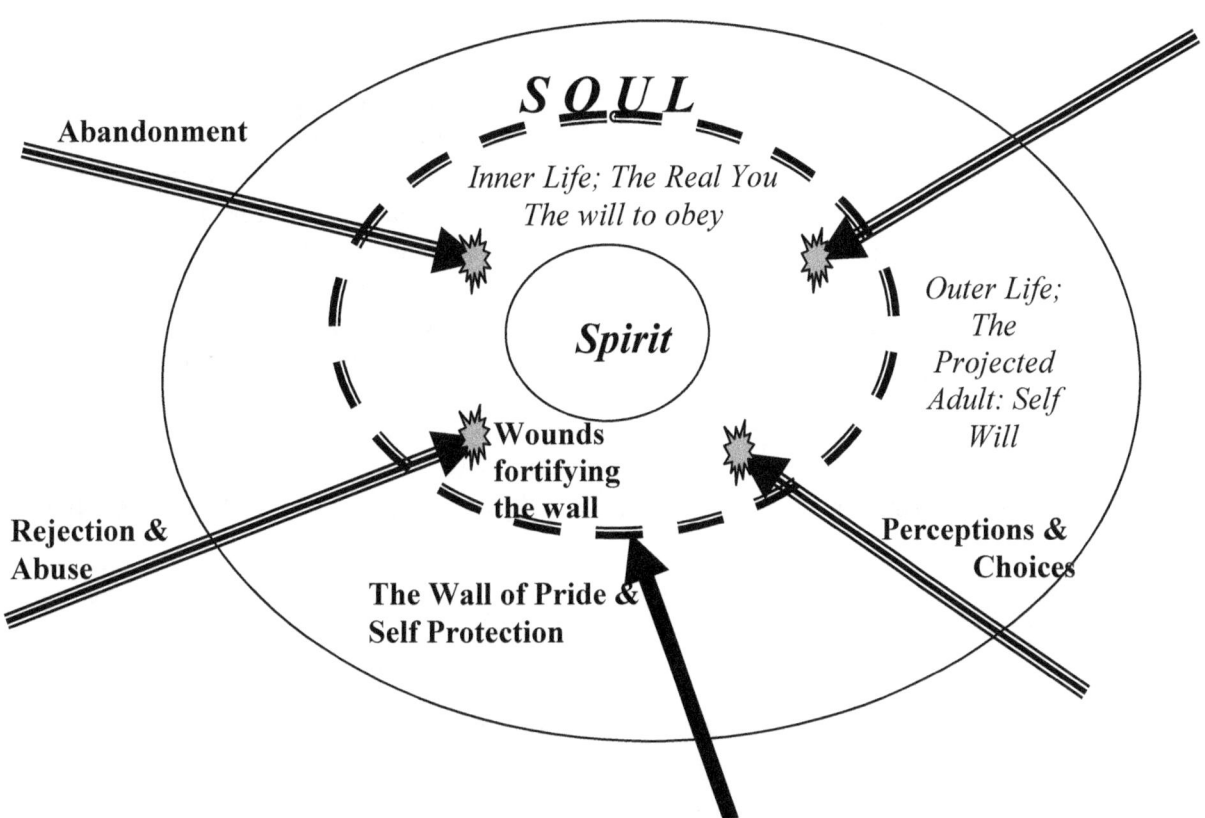

*When Rejection is present within the life,
A person will respond by seeking to protect him/herself,
from further injury; hiding behind a wall of Pride.
Every wound is countered with a pursuit by the personality
to find acceptance. Behind the wall of Pride, (or emotional
"fig leaves," if you will)
The infection grows within,
bruising everything as it gains space.
The person has ceased emotional development
at the time of life when injury was received within the soul.*

He/She cannot grow beyond the wall.

Rejection shows itself in: insecurity, timidity, shyness, a sense of worthlessness and futility, inability to give or receive love, unforgiveness, the accounting of wrongs suffered. The defensive and accusing response to correction, suspicion. Seeds of bitterness; Lack of trust or Close relationship. The inability to have long-term relationships, or stay in one place for a long time. Fear of relationships, low esteem of purpose, isolation. Inability to accept physical characteristics. A sense of not belonging. Bitterness. Anger. Inability to receive correction or instruction. It is the seedbed for rebellion. Over-achievement can be the result of a quest for acceptance and worth.

With what elements of the description of Rejection can you identify? Write them here.

___

___

What experiences do you remember in your lifetime, when these qualities of Rejection were given place?

___

___

Is Rejection a "generational" quality within your family?

___

___

In what ways can you now see it's characteristics being passed down from generation to generation in your family line?

___

___

2. When Rejection's presence is felt within a person's life, the result is "fig leaf" behavior within the soul. The person seeks to cover the hurt, utilizing a mannerism or behavior pattern to protect the person from becoming vulnerable again. These protective measures find their strength within the person's own abilities and strengths, rather than from the nature of the Holy Spirit. Thus, their roots spring from the qualities of Pride.

Pride	**will** cause:	Trust in self, overconfident in the flesh (emotional and spiritual), ambition to prove worth, insensitivity to others, judges hastily, sharp words, competitive, seeks independence, seeds of anxiety and depression. Stubbornness. Selfishness, Self-advancement, the focus upon personal rights and desires. The quest for self-gratification, discontentment, covetousness, jealousy. The indulgence of personal rights and feelings. The denial of any need for change, healing or freedom. Inner blindness and inability to hear the voice of Father God. Shame motivated. Ruled by the fear of man-- "what will people think?" Identity is peer based, rather than God-based.

With what elements of the description of Pride can you identify? Write them here.

_____

What experiences do you remember in your lifetime, when these qualities of Pride were given place?

_____

_____

Is Pride a "generational" quality within your family? In what way?

_____

How has your life been wounded by Pride?

_____

_____

3. The practice of seeking to heal oneself without the power of Creator God or the Blood of Jesus must be recognized as sin. It is trusting in counterfeit provision, and must be repented of. Write a prayer of confession and repentance on these lines, acknowledging those places where you have trusted in your own abilities and strengths to heal and shield your soul, rather than upon the Unconditional Love and Provision of Jesus Christ.

_____

_____

_____

_____

_____

_____

Rejection pushes a person down,
causing them to believe they are without value, and are unimportant

Pride puffs a person up,
causing them to believe they are perfect and unimpeachable

Abba Father desires us to become free from both

That freedom allows us to develop and grow
with the personal identity He has call us to develop
For His purpose and Plan.

Bruises of Rejection

Rejection brings:

The continually negative focus of life, which causes a person to be consumed with their own needs and struggles; A constant draw for attention and acceptance; Low esteem of their purpose in God's eyes; Always looking for better days, past or present; Difficulty accepting physical characteristics. Those who bear the weight of rejection, tend to put an unreasonable burden upon those around them, needing to be "carried" day-to-day, afraid to face difficulties in life alone.

A person who suffers from Rejection, always feels as though they are on the outside looking in when it comes to relationships. They are afraid to trust their heart to another person. Most always, have a deep, insatiable need for affirmation and praise, allowing the words and opinions of others to provide their own sense of security. The person lives in a quest for acceptance. It is easier for them to receive rejection than acceptance and love; totally self-centered, they move from one close relationship to another, never able to maintain a long-term relationship. May even turn to animals for acceptance, or to the acquisition of material goods, seeking to fill inner emptiness with material possessions, or food.

Rejection creates the desire to control in order to prevent coming under control and experiencing the repetition of a hurt; The inability to voluntarily submit to God-placed authorities, or receive correction, without justifying or comparing one's own attitude or behavior with that of another.

The Evidence of Rejection's Influence in Emotional Development

Emotional Immaturity (development stopped at maturity level bruise was received)

Self-Pity, Insecurity, feelings of Insignificance, a sense of having no personal value or worth

Loneliness, Fears of being rejected, Vanity --looks for things to fill the hole inside

Sets unreasonable goals for self, and then drives self to achieve, code of perfectionism

Function has replaced affection and heart-to-heart communication

There is difficulty in understanding and entering into what the Bible calls "kinship" -- close relationship with others, with no barriers of protection

A cycle of performance/discouragement/depression (more and more is piled upon the soul until the person "cracks" under the strain)

Ruled by the Fear of Man, Fear of Rejection, and the Wall of Pride

An inability to really receive love, letting your heart feel it and enjoy it

Which of these characteristics do you see in your own life?

_____

_____

_____

_____

Without the intervention of God's Spirit, Rejection will open door to bondage.

> **Please listen to the tenth CD, utilizing your notebook, for Session Ten**
>
> **"How Abba Father Develops Character"**
> **before you move ahead**

Notes:

A Second Chance at a First Choice

When the children of Israel left Egypt, they had not whole-heartedly decided to let go of the gods of Egypt. They had brought with them the symbols of foreign gods, and practices from Egyptian idolatry. You know, the things they weren't willing to let go of …… yet; things which still held their attention and their allegiance.

It was kind of like holding an ace-in-the-hole. If God didn't work out, they could always go back.

It had been forty years since the "slave generation" had decided not to take what God had offered them. Forty years since Moses, with a heavy heart, and had turned them around and go back into the desert.

                              Forty long years.

In all that time, Abba Father had not forsaken them. Their shoes had not shown any wear. Their clothes lasted like iron -- (perhaps so they could get a picture of the unseen material they had chosen to clothe their souls with.) He had sent manna for forty years --every morning, just like clockwork.

                              Over and over again He proved His faithfulness to them.

And, also,
over and over again,
they showed their distrust and stubbornness to Him.

But He still loved them. He still wanted His people to live in the Promised Land.

Eventually, every person who had made the choice not to receive the Promise died.

       And with them, the yearnings for other gods died.
              The allegiance to other things to comfort them lost its hold.
                      The only God who remained true was the Father.

They could see that now.

Moses had lost his temper and vented his flesh in disobedience. He would not go into the land. The Father would take him home. Moses needed the rest. He had believed the promise, but his patience had worn thin.

Their children lived.
        Joshua and Caleb lived.
                These would be the ones who would take the land.

They had believed from the beginning.

Joshua stood on the same hill where he had stood so many years before. He looked out over the camp. He was waiting for his spies to return.

Just three weeks before, while they were camped at Shittim, he had sent two men secretly into Jericho.

"Go, view the land, especially Jericho," he had told them. He was expecting them to return any time.

It had been an eventful month. God had spoken to him, and chosen him to lead the people into the Promised Land.

> "Moses, the servant of the Lord, is dead now. It is time to rise up and cross the Jordan, and take possession of the land I am giving to you. No one will be able to stop you. Do not be afraid, for I will be with you.
>
> "Be strong and courageous. Be careful to keep my commandments, and walk in them. Do not tremble or be afraid. I am with you wherever you go."

Joshua had then spoken to the people. There would have to be a choice made. He spoke to them.

"The Lord your God gives you rest, and will give you this land."

He had been blessed by their response. "Whatever you tell us, we will do, and wherever you send us, we will go. We will obey you in everything."

They had learned a lot in forty years of wandering. They were tired of just existing in a desert environment.

Joshua aimed a stone at a nearby tree. How close could he get to that knot? He threw. The stone bounced off the tree bark. Pretty close. He looked down into the valley.

Two figures were approaching. He waited to be sure he knew them.

Yes. They were his men. Joshua ran down the road to meet them. "How did it go?"

"There is much to tell you. We met a woman named Rahab who helped us a great deal. We promised her that when we take the city, she and her family will be spared. She believed in our God. She hid us in her home, and protected us when the rulers of the city came looking for us. Her house is inside the wall of the city, with a window which looks to the outside, so she let us down by a rope. She told us to go to the hill country and to hide there until they stopped looking for us. And here we are.."

Joshua had many questions. "What is the attitude toward us in Jericho? They must know we are here."

"The men in the city are afraid of us because of our God. They have no courage to fight us. They have heard about the parting of the Red Sea, and of the battles we won against huge armies under Moses' leadership, and they are terrified."

This was great; really wonderful! Everything the Father had said was true!!

Joshua slept well that night. In the morning, he sent officers through the camp, telling the people to prepare themselves to go into the land. But the preparation was not one for battle. It was a time of consecration to the Father.

A time for preparation of heart to obey;

fully obey.

They crossed the Jordan River the next morning. It was at flood stage, and rushing over its banks. But the choice had been made to obey fully. So, the priests stepped into the water. When their feet touched the water, they looked at each other. The river stopped, and the water created a wall on one side of them.

Everyone crossed over on dry ground.

This was their Red Sea experience.

They built an altar on the other side.

The soldiers in Jericho shook with fear. This was no ordinary God. These were no ordinary people. They took small comfort in the thickness of their double-walled city. What was coming?

Rahab called her family together, and invited as many as could squeeze into her tiny townhouse to come in to her house.

Come in with the believer, and live.

Not too many days later, the Lord spoke to Joshua.

"I have given Jericho into your hands, along with its king and all its valiant warriors.

"Take the Ark of the Covenant, and put seven priests who carry ram's horn trumpets in front of it. March around the city, all the men of war circling the city one time. Do this for six days in silence.

"Then, on the seventh day, march around the city seven times, and the priests will blow the trumpets. When the people hear the trumpets, they are to shout with a great shout, and the wall will fall down flat."

He also instructed them not to leave anything alive in Jericho; not even the animals.

                            Everything infected with sin had to die.

Joshua instructed the people to do as the Lord had commanded. Talk about unusual military strategy!!

And even though it was not understood in the physical realm, something was happening in the unseen, spiritual realm. Those circlings of the city were binding something up, and causing it to be unable to lash out at them.

Jericho was the symbol of power in this new land. It's fortresses and walls were the mightiest and least penetrable. So, Abba Father was leading Joshua to take the most powerful ruler down first.
                    Their marches were binding up the strongman.
                    They were rendering powerless the ruling spiritual force of darkness
                        which had held that region of the land for so long.

The Father was opening the door to **all** of the rest of the victories they would savor in the years ahead.

As they marched, silently, they chose to say nothing but what the Father had told them to say.

Then, as they shouted, they praised Him in the midst of the battle, knowing victory was promised and sure. When the walls fell, they were faithful to the command, dealing a death blow to everything within that had sworn allegiance to Jericho. It was a conquered place. It now belonged to Abba Father, and his Joshua.

After all, the first stronghold to fall is the hardest one to pull down.

                And the Father did battle for them--

                        As they chose to obey.

> **Please listen to the eleventh CD, utilizing your notebook, for Session Eleven**
>
> **""My Jericho and Promised Land"
> before you move ahead**

Notes:

Rejection's Supporting Players

Bitterness, An evidence of Rejection in the Soul

The condition of the soul holding to a hurt received; The absence of forgiveness. The person hides behind isolation; operating with a critical nature, insensitive to other people. (The real purpose of criticism: To lower the reputation of those persons whose influence intimidates the embittered person, in order to cause their low esteem to exceed the damaged reputation.)

(Hebrew)   "mar" = Bitterness, hatred
(Greek)   "pikria" = Bitterness, hatred

1. Bitterness is discontentment   I Samuel 22:2

In what areas of your life have you allowed your heart to become discontent?

_____

_____

Write out I Timothy 6:6 here.

_____

_____

_____

Contentment = "autarkeia" (Greek), meaning, a perfect condition of life in which no aid or support is needed, a sufficiency of the necessities of life, a mind contented with its lot. This word is translated "sufficiency" in II Corinthians 9:8.

Write out II Corinthians 9:8 here.

_____

Can you believe that Father God desires to provide you with contentment? _____

Confess your difficulty with your circumstances in life here.

_____
–

_____
–

2. Bitterness seeps down into the heartJeremiah 4:18

3. Bitterness causes complaining and turmoilJob 7:11 and Job 3:20-26

In what ways have you allowed your heart to become bitter?

What things do you find yourself complaining about?

_____
–

4. Bitterness robs the enjoyment of mealtimesJob 21:25

5. Bitterness causes weepingI Samuel 1:10

6. Bitterness can lead to a desire to dieJob 10:1

7. In this condition, death is bitterI Samuel 15:22
Job 21:25

What situations in your life are bitter to you?

In what ways do you feel rejected?

8. Bitter words are armed words (doing injury) Psalm 64:3

9. Words spoken in bitterness plant seeds in others, Hebrews 12:15
which grow into bitterness in their hearts,
making them defiled in God's sight.

10. Cursing accompanies bitterness Romans 3:14

What bitter words have you allowed to lodge in your heart?

_____

_____

Speak out those words to Father God, as a confession. "Father, I remember when (a person) said, "_____" to me. I repent for allowing those words to lodge within my heart, and cause me to become bitter. I break the power of those words over my life, and I give those words to you, Lord. Please heal me." Repeat this process with each wound of bitterness the enemy has brought about in your soul.

11. Bitterness causes wandering. Isaiah 38:14
(The inability to stay in one church, or keep a Job 3:26
job for a long time, or even stay in one town).

Do you find yourself wandering? Do you have an inability to rest? _____

12. Bitterness comes when a person walks away from the Lord   Jeremiah 2:19

If you have walked away from the Father in any area of your life, write out a prayer of repentance here.

_____

_____

13. Bitterness causes a curse upon a person's life   Numbers 5:18-24

Are there any areas of your life in which you have watched the Father's blessings fade away? In what ways could bitterness be attached to those areas?

_____

_____

14. The bondage of iniquity causes bitterness　　　　　　　　　Acts 8:23
*(iniquities --guilt and tendencies to sin,
which are inherent in our fleshly nature.
Generational weaknesses -- See Exodus 34:7,
Numbers 14:18, and Lamentations 5:7)*

1. Write out a prayer, asking forgiveness for allowing yourself to live with bitterness.

2. Also in the prayer, break any generational tie to bitterness in your family. Name those who you know were bitter in nature, and cut off any generational heritage or soul-tie to that person. Repent in proxy (see Nehemiah 1:5-9) for their sin, asking forgiveness.

3. Ask the Father to cover that area in the Blood of Jesus, which will bring spiritual life and understanding to those things which have been functioning under the curse of Death brought on my bitterness. Thank you for your freedom.

Suspicion, An Evidence of Rejection in the Soul

The thought processes of false accusation. The inability to trust others, for fear of repeating a hurt already received at another time. The dissection of the motives and actions of others, giving way to criticism and resentment.

Suspicion is Satan's counterfeit for the Holy Spirit's ministry of Discernment.

1. Suspicion led to Miriam's sin of gossip, rebellion   Numbers 12:1-16
    and judgment of leprosy.

Miriam and Aaron most probably felt replaced in their relationship with Moses, by Moses' wife. As Moses' wife, this woman would hear about Moses' experiences firsthand, and would know his heart. She might have even been asked by her husband to help with the huge task of caring for the Israelite women. Perhaps Moses asked her to do something which Miriam had previously done. The Bible does not say. But it does say that Miriam and Aaron became critical of leadership and family. In any close relationship in which this type of situation occurred, it would be normal to deal with feelings of rejection. But Miriam and Aaron, because they also shared in Moses' ministry, took issue with Moses, who was walking in scriptural one-ness with his wife.

Because of the manner in which the Lord dealt with the situation, it is obvious that Miriam is the one who had the original problem. She allowed it to "eat away" at her soul, until it affected an entire nation. The consequence for her attitude was that Father God allowed her to see visibly what her suspicion and criticism had done in the invisible realm.

In what ways have suspicion and criticism "eaten away" at your own soul?

_____

Have you been rejected by someone, and now have difficulty trusting your heart to those around you? Where and when was the wall erected?

_____

_____

In what areas would you like to repent and ask for cleansing from suspicion and a critical nature?

_____

2. Suspicion led to King Saul's attempt to murder David.   I Samuel 22:6-8

Father God had pronounced blessings upon David. He had triumphed over Goliath, been anointed by Samuel as the next king, and the presence of God's Spirit followed whenever he played his harp and worshipped the Lord. He moved in the anointing. In contrast, Saul had lost the blessings of Father God due to his disobedience (I Samuel 15), and the kingdom of Israel was taken away from him. The Spirit of the Lord had departed from him (see 1 Samuel 16:14-23), and he suffered torment due to his negligent choices.

It is very easy to fall into the trap the enemy was set for Saul. When we see those who have more of the blessings of the Lord than we do --more anointing, more giftedness, more favor --we assume that Father God somehow loves them more than He loves us. We look upon them as though they have what we should have, and become suspicious of their motives - when usually, watching what is happening in others' lives is unknowingly and unintentionally drawing our own of Rejection *to* the surface.

In what ways have your compared yourself with other Christians, and concluded that somehow you must be less in Father God's eyes than they are?

_____
-
_____
-

What choices have you made that could have stopped the blessings of the Lord upon your life?

_____
-
_____
-

Write out a prayer of confession of your fear and insecurity regarding your place before Father God here.

_____
-

3. Suspicion led to Joseph's servitude in Egypt.   Genesis 37:5-30

Joseph's brothers' misunderstanding, and subsequently their suspicion and judgment of his dreams and destiny, caused them to sell him into bondage in Egypt. As a result, he was humiliated by his own earthly family, forsaken by all who knew him, falsely accused in Egypt, imprisoned unjustly for years, and finally saw the fulfillment of his God-given dreams.

In what ways have you been injured by the suspicion and criticism of other people?

_____
_

_____
_

Read Genesis 50:1.5-21. This indicates the heart of Joseph toward his brothers in response to their humiliating treatment, suspicion, and jealousies. Write out a prayer of consecration of your own places of rejection because of suspicion here.

_____
_

_____
_

Suspicion is a form of silent accusation. Write out Revelation 12:10-11 here.

_____
_

_____
_

According to this scripture, where does accusation, even silent accusation, originate?

_____
_

_____
_

Write out a prayer of repentance and confession to the Father for the times you have entered into the sins of accusation and suspicion, neglecting to allow His love to be shed abroad in your own heart. (See Romans 5:5)

_____

_____

_____

Self-Condemnation, An Evidence of Rejection in the Soul

I The constant lack of acceptance of a person's own humanness; Self-hatred, Self-rejection; The inability to enjoy spiritual blessings; The continual looking for "what did wrong;" The constant cycle of performance. The inability to learn from mistakes and press on with living --the collection of mistakes and failures or even wrongs suffered as "evidence" against the purpose of God upon the person's life.

1. Even when righteous, this heart condemns a person   Job 9:20

2. Even when innocent, this heart will declare guilt.   Job 9:20

In what ways do you find yourself taking blame for the circumstances around you, and the attitudes of other people?

_____

_____

When Jesus Christ lives within your heart, the Father sees you as a righteous person, through the Blood of the Lamb. In what ways do you find yourself arguing with this provision, or seeking to nullify it?

_____

_____

Write out Ephesians 2:4-6 here.

_____

_____

_____

Does this scripture include you?

3. When we carry iniquities, we store up guilt upon ourselves   Matthew 23:31-32

**Iniquities are the weaknesses and tendencies to sin, many times inherited and are inherent in us when we are born. When we cover those with the denials of pride, we heap upon our own lives the fruits of self-condemnation. (Note: In order for Adam and Eve to be covered by Father God in sin's expulsion from the Garden of Eden, the coverings of fig leaves they had made for themselves had to be removed.
See Genesis 3:7 and 3:21)**

What inherent traits to sin have you sought to hide from the family of God, bringing condemnation upon yourself?

_____

_____

4. The fruit of judging others is self-condemnation   Romans 2: 1

We open ourselves up to judgment from others and from our own hearts when we fall into the trap of passing judgment upon other people. People, who many times are seeking to become all that Jesus wants them to be as well, but making mistakes and sometimes failing, as we all do.

Write out Matthew 7:1 _____

_____

In what ways have you allowed yourself to judge other people?

_____

_____

II Corinthians 10:12 tells us the fruit of comparing our lives with the lives of other people. Write that scripture out here.

_____

_____

Write out a prayer, asking for forgiveness for judging others here.

_____

_____

_____

_____

Fear, the Evidence of Rejection within the Soul

The "cloud" or "fog" which convinces the heart of the immenseness of its enemy, and the futility of seeking to fight back; The threat of retribution in the event of victory; The threat of the loss of loved ones, or impending danger; Triggered by situations, relationships, and circumstances. Immobilizes the person and can lead to the bondage of Fear; Fear cannot be reasoned with.

1.. Fear is not of God.   II Timothy 1:7
    a. He has given us power
    b. He has given us love
    c. He has given us a sound mind

What fears do you battle? _____

2. Believing and accepting the   Romans 10:17
Love of God (faith in Him)
is the answer to fear.

When we choose what we will believe, we choose either fear, or faith. Faith works through the love of God. (See Galatians 5:6 and Ephesians 6:23). Whenever you battle with fear, sing a song of praise regarding the love of God, and your fear will disappear. Write out I Corinthians 13:4-7 here, and then memorize it.

_____

_____

3. Perfect love casts out fear.   I John 4:18

The love of Father God is perfect. Write out those things that bring fear to your life, and then pray the prayer on the page following this lesson. Write out Romans 5:8-9 here, and then memorize it.

_____

_____

(Note: There is a demonic fear which torments and attacks during vulnerable moments, such as when a person is trying to sleep, impairing judgments and perception. This fear cannot be reasoned with, or disciplined. It must be cast out through the Name and Blood of Jesus Christ.)

A Scripture-Based Prayer
To Help in Overcoming Fear

*"There is no fear in love; but perfect love casts out fear;
because fear has torment. He that fears is not
made perfect in love." I John 4: 18*

**When fear is present in a person's life, it is an indication of an area
where the love of Father God has not been fully received and applied.
The unconditional love and acceptance of God is the only thing able to remove
fear from the human heart.**

**Fear cannot be reasoned with –
it must be confronted and commanded to leave
with the Word of God and prayer.**

Pray this prayer out loud each time you find yourself doing battle with Fear.

Father God, I confess my fear to you. It is my choice to confront my fear with your Word and to command it to go from my life in the name of Jesus Christ, my Savior.

Lord, I confess that your Word says that you have not given me a spirit of fear, but of power, love and a sound mind. You have not given me a spirit of bondage, but you have adopted me and made me your own child. You have promised that no evil will befall me, and no plague will come near my dwelling place. You have given your angels charge of me,to keep me in all of my ways. You desire to be my confidence, and to keep my foot from even slipping in the path you are leading me. You will keep me from oppression and terror, and establish me in righteousness.

I confess that you are my Helper. You are my light and my salvation. You are the strength of my life. You are the strength of my heart, and I choose to put my hope in You. Abba Father, I receive your love for me. I choose to open every part of my life to your love and care. Let your perfect love cast out all fear from me.

Father, I know that nothing can separate me from Your love for me; not tribulation, or distress, or persecution, of famine, or need, or peril, or violence. You have made me to be a conqueror over all of these things. You always love me. In every area, in every situation, you love me, without change. Nothing can separate me from your love --not death, not life, not angels, not demonic principalities, no power on earth, nothing in this present life, or in the life to come. Nothing can separate me from your love for me. You are always with me, even until the end of the earth. When I pass through waters, I will not be overwhelmed.

When I pass through rivers, they will not sweep over me. When I pass through fire, I will not be burned, for you are my Savior.

You are with me, so I will not be dismayed. You are my God and you have promised to help me, strengthen me, and uphold me with your righteous right hand. You preserve me from trouble and sing songs of deliverance over my life. You deliver me from all of my fears. I will trust in you. You are my refuge and fortress. You have promised to rescue me from evil. You have promised to come and save me. You have promised to contend with those that contend with me, and to save my children. You have promised that no weapon formed against me will prosper, and every tongue that rises up against me will be condemned. You have promised to strengthen me by Your Spirit with might in the inner man.

I plead the covering of the Blood of the Lamb over my soul. Fear, you have no authority in speak into my life, or to influence me. I will stand firm and see the deliverance the Lord has for me. I do not even have to fight this battle, for the battle is not mine, but it belongs to God. You have been defeated by the death of the Son of God, and I will not give you place any longer. I stand firm in the Love of my Heavenly Father.

Isaiah 41:10-13	Romans 8:15	Isaiah 43:1-3	Isaiah 41:10
Philippians 1:28	Psalm 27:1	Psalm 91:1,4-7	Psalm 91:10-11
Isaiah 54:14	Hebrews 13:6	Psalm 31:24	Exodus 14:13
Deuteronomy 31:6-8	Proverbs 3:25-26	Romans 8:29,31	Psalm 27:1-3
II Chronicles 20:15	II Timothy 1:7	Isaiah 12:2	
Romans 8:35-39			

Deception!

"It will work. Just try it."

"I'm doing the best I can!"

There. What else can you think of?"

The men had finished sewing patches on their clothes and sandals. For over a week now, their wives had held on to bread provisions, so they would appear to be old and crusty.

"I hope it works. It's our only hope."

"Do I look like an ambassador to you?"

"Well, you'll do. We have to try."

They set out on their journey. It would take less than a day to get to Gilgal.

Joshua and his generals were seated around the fire. Plans and strategies were being worked out for the next steps in taking possession of the land. The Lord was leading them. These were good days.

He stoked the fire with a nearby stick. Looking up at the smoke trail, he noticed travelers approaching. They looked tired. They had come a long way.

"Greetings!" he called out. "Where have you come from?"

They looked at each other and answered. "We have come from a very far country because we have heard of the fame of your God, and all He did for you in Egypt."

"Come and sit with us by the fire and warm yourselves."

The Gibeonites sighed with relief. They were in. This was the first step.

"What can we do for you?" Joshua asked.

"Well, we heard you were in the land. Our elders, and all the inhabitants of our country spoke to us and said, 'Take provisions in your hand for the journey, and go to meet them, and say to them,

> 'We are your servants; now then, make a deal with us.

'Look at this bread. It was warm when we left home, and now it is dry and crusty Our clothes were new, and now they are worn, because of our long journey. Our wineskins were new, and now they are torn.

'We will not harm you. Please let us live."

Joshua and his generals did not ask the Lord for counsel. Moved to pity in the very depths of their souls, by what they saw and heard, their hearts filled with sympathy for these poor men, and they drew up a contract with them. They made peace with them. They would allow them to live.

They didn't know these were their enemies.
        It seemed good – just like Eve in Eden….

        They didn't know…….

Now the land would never be really free from the effects of the former occupants. It would never totally belong to Israel.

It wasn't until three days later that Joshua learned the truth. They came into the land of Gibeon, to take possession and do battle. But they could not do it. They had given their word.

        They had been deceived.
            They had made a deal with the enemy.

In the end, the Gibeonites became slaves to Israel. Joshua could not break his word and kill them. To enslave them was the only way that Joshua felt he could in some way come close to keeping the commandment of the Lord to do away with every sin in the land...

        at least they wouldn't be free to do any damage.

    But now --

        Their influence remained, and it was now in their homes and families, serving them…...

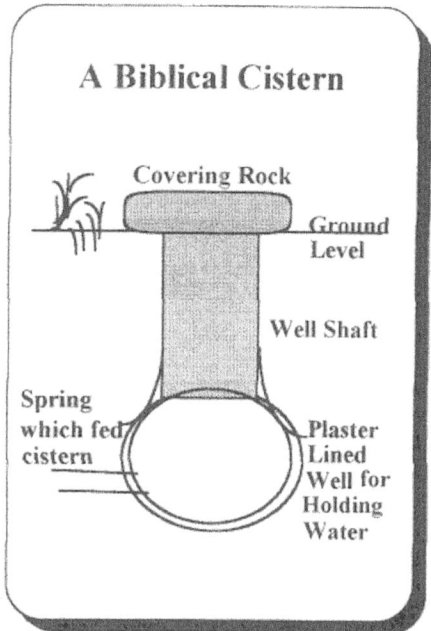

A Biblical Cistern

What is a Broken Cistern?

"But whosoever drinks of the water that J shall give him shall never thirst; but the water that I shall give him shall be in him a well of water springing up into everlasting life." John 4:14

When Jesus spoke these words in John 4:14, He was speaking to a woman in Samaria, who had come to a well to draw water. Because of the construction of the Biblical well, or cistern, it was easy for her to understand what He meant by the words "well of water springing up into everlasting life."

The well, or cistern was usually scooped out of the earth, and lined with plaster, or dug out in a rock with a lining added, for the purpose of catching and holding rain water for later use. Many cisterns were spring fed, and thus always held fresh water. In the country, especially the wilderness, a man who dug a cistern would hide its entrance with a large stone or rock, rolled over the top, in order to prevent animals, or even other people from falling *in* as they walked by unawares.

During their travels in the wilderness, the Israelites had no wells from which to draw their water. The people would carry the water they needed with them in *skins* as they traveled from place to place, and when they camped, water was always a consideration. For this reason, it became the dream of every Israelite man to "draw water from his own cistern," meaning each home would have its own water supply. Obviously, a spring fed cistern was the best quality source for water, since *it* was not dependent upon rainfall.

Sometimes the lining of a cistern would crack or break, due to any number of circumstances, and the well would no longer be able to store water. The well would then be abandoned, and another would dug for use in its place. It was abandoned wells, or cisterns, such as this, that held Joseph in Genesis 37:22, and Jeremiah in Jeremiah 38:6. Such a "prison" proved fatal for many.

There is an understanding within the Scripture, that a well-watered location was called an "oasis" in the desert, and was known to be a place of health, rest and blessing. (See Jeremiah 31:12 and Isaiah 58:11)

Proverbs 22:15 speaks of the man who gives ("watereth") also receiving blessing ("shall be watered"). Jesus speaks to the Samaritan woman at the well, and offers her eternal life, promising to be a spring-fed well within her --a source of health and blessing. Later, in John 7:37-38, Jesus says that anyone who thirsts, and comes to Him, will experience rivers of living water flowing from within his spirit.

There is, for each of us a believers, the availability to a Spring-fed Well, which will not only water our souls, bringing health, rest, and blessing, but will then become a river of living water, which will then affect the lives of everyone we touch.

    Jesus Christ is the DaySpring (Luke 1:78-80), and He is the Source of this Life.

However, a difficulty exists. In the world, we find ourselves living in today's realities,
        when divorce is rampant,
            abuse is pandemic,
                selfishness and anger are prevalent
                      death is seen everywhere

and what used to be considered "normal life", is not "normal" anymore --

when 8 out of 10 children graduate from high school with a different family structure than the structure into which they were born --

when 3 out of 5 women are sexually abused or violated before the age of 15 –

when 43% of women have experienced an abortion, and of that 43%, 80% have experienced it more than one time,

when 67% of young men within our culture grow up without a positive biological role model.

When 85% of families have fragmented lifestyles – many not even eating meals together –

    when honesty and integrity are laughed at more than ever before --

It is not surprising that within many of us, the inner lining of the soul has cracked, and they find themselves unable to hold on to hope, or joy, or peace.

Such a person sees more stony places in their souls than they see blessing. Life has lost its strength and purpose. Existing seems to be the only thing they have left. They are not quitters --but they don't think they have the energy to try.

Going along for the ride appears to be the only way to get through each day.

    This is the description of the broken spirit.

Perhaps you have just depended upon the water to fall into your life from those around you, wetting down the stony places with what flowed from within their lives ---or maybe you hang on desperately for just on~ good "splash" every once in a while --just so you don't forget what the Presence of a Loving God is really like.

or maybe you can't remember --its been too long –

you've tried to make repairs on the walls of your soul that determine your identity, but it just doesn't seem to "hold water."

Understand this –Abba Father God has not given up on you. He wants to help you.

And, before you can even make an effort to engage your will to fight --

>You must come to Him --
>>The Creator, Designer --
>>>And Healer of Your Soul --

For a new cistern. It will become in you a well springing up unto eternal life.

> *"Says the Lord they have forsaken me, the fountain of living waters,*
> *and hewed them out cisterns, broken cisterns that can hold no water."*
> *Jeremiah 2: 12b &13*

The Steps to a Broken Spirit

"The Lord is near to the brokenhearted, and saves those who are crushed in spirit." Psalm 34: 18

1. In Matthew 13:3-9, Jesus tells a parable of a man who went out to scatter seed on a field. In Bible times, the farmers would hand scatter their seed, from a seed-bag hung over the shoulder. In the story Jesus told, he describes the experience this particular man had, and the different places in which the seeds landed when they fell? List the four different sites given in the story here.

    1. _____

    2. _____

    3. _____

    4. _____

2. What happened to each set of seeds?

    1. _____

    2. _____

    3. _____

    4. _____

3. In Matthew 13:18-23, Jesus then gives the meaning behind the parable He has given. In Mark4:14, another account of the same story, He tells what the seed represents. What is the seed?_____

4. The different types of soil represent varying conditions of the human heart. In the parable, what are the enemies of God's Word within the heart in each instance? How do they stop the person from growing spiritually?

    1. _____

    2. _____

    3. _____

    4. _____

5. What reason does Jesus give in Matthew 13:10-15 for teaching the people in such a cryptic way? What does He tell the disciples is the general condition of those in the crowd listening?

_____
___

6. Using the following Scriptures, categorize the condition of the soil of your own heart;

      a. Working too hard, striving in your own   Ecclesiastes 2:4-12
          strength for accomplishments.   Ecclesiastes 2:17
          This brings despair upon the heart.   Ecclesiastes 2:20-23

This scripture describes a heart with _____ soil.

      b. The heart is weakened by false doctrines,   Hebrews 13:9
      but strengthened by the grace of God. (False
      doctrines could include legalistic beliefs,
      "flaky spirituality", as well as false religions.)

This scripture describes a heart with _____ soil.

      c. Sorrow breaks the spirit.   Proverbs 15:13
      d. Heaviness accompanies sorrow.   Romans 9:2

This scripture describes a heart with _____ soil.

      e. Anxiety held within causes depression,   Proverbs 12:25
      or heaviness. "heaviness" = worry or
      anxiety "stoop" = depression

This scripture describes a heart with _____ soil.

      f. Sexual sin (sex outside of marriage) destroys   Proverbs 6:32
      the soul. It creates a spiritual and emotional attachment
      between the parties involved.

(This is also an open door for torment, depending   Mark 10:6-8
upon what condition of spirit the other person is in.   I Corinthians 6:16
It's power over the life must be broken by repentance,   Genesis 2:24
confession and prayer. See scriptural example in
Genesis 34:1-3)

This scripture describes a heart with _____ soil.

      g. Hope deferred causes sickness in the heart.   Proverbs 13:12
      "deferred" = prolonged, postponed, or scattered
      (The putting off of the fulfillment of a
      promise made, unattainable but reasonable goals).

This scripture describes a heart with _____ soil.

      h. Drinking alcohol destroys the soul.   **Hosea 4:11**

This scripture describes a heart with _____ soil

      i. Envy in the heart causes it to be unsound.   Proverbs 14:30
      [The fear of the Lord washes the envy of
      sinners from the soul. (Proverbs 23:17)]

      j. Accepting bribes corrupts the heart.   Ecclesiastes 7:7

This scripture describes a heart with _____ soil.

7. With which conditions of the soil of the human heart do you identify?

_____
___

_____
___

Steps to Healing the Spirit

*"Beloved, I pray that in all things you would prosper
and be in health, even as thy soul prospers." III John 2*

1. Realize that you cannot heal yourself   Proverbs 20:9
                                                                                           Ecclesiastes 7:20

2. Healing is received when we open the broken areas   Isaiah 61:1
to the Father, and allow Him to bind up (idea of a
splint, and bandage) the hurts.

A broken spirit is the end result of allowing your heart to accommodate things which compete for your relationship with Father God. When a heart has been trodden down, (like a road), it must receive softening with the Word of God. In Ephesians 5:26, Paul tells us that Christ will cleanse His church with the Water of the Word. Write out the promise for this condition of heart that is found in Isaiah 44:3 here.

_____
____

_____
____

_____
____

_____
____

Hardness of heart can come from the experience of bitter circumstances, or just simply from receiving injury. Allow the Lord to wash these hurts from your life, and bind up your wounds. Just ask Him.

Write here what Father God promises in the first part of Jeremiah 30:17.

_____
___

_____
___

3. The heart is strengthened by grace   Hebrews 13:9
     a. The choice must be made to release
         the ones who injured your soul.   Matthew 18:21-35
     b. The choice must be made to forgive
         the ones who injured your soul.   Matthew 6:14-15

Unforgiveness stems from a hard heart. Unforgiveness and stubbornness are characterized by a stoniness which resides within the heart. This quality only shows itself at certain times, or when particular subjects arise. (It can show itself in prejudice.) What is the conditional promise regarding our own forgiveness, given in Matthew 6:15? Write it out here.

_____

4. Healing is received by receiving (listening with openness and trust) to instruction and correction.　　　Proverbs 15:19

5. Healing is received when we are obedient to the Word of God.　　　Matthew 11:29
    (In contrast, being disobedient to the
    Word will weaken the inner man.
    This means any area --from prayer to tithing.)

The Word of God can be rendered powerless within a person's life by Satan's plots and schemes. He will do anything and everything he can to dilute the power of Father God's principles and promises, through intimidation, doubt, and even accusation against the one bringing the teaching to the person's ears. Are there any areas of your heart where the Word of God might have been reduced to a mental exercise, rather than a life-changing event, due to Satan's activities? Write them here.

_____

_____

_____

6. Healing is received by seeking the wisdom of God.　　　Proverbs 19:8

7. Healing is received by doing what is acceptable to God.　　　Ecclesiastes 9:7

8. Healing is received when we allow the heart to be merry. It works like medicine.　　　Proverbs 17:22

Write out Proverbs 4:23 here _____

_____

The Choice to Live in Freedom

Where will you walk?

"And if it seem evil unto you to serve the Lord, <u>choose you this day whom ye will serve:</u> whether the gods which your fathers served that were on the other side of the flood (demonic bondage- see Genesis 6), or the gods of the Amorites (serving fleshly appetites), in whose land ye dwell:

<u>BUT AS FOR ME AND MY HOUSE</u>

<u>WE WILL SERVE THE LORD."</u>

Joshua 24:15

Many times, when a person has received prayer for deliverance over an area in his or her life, they will sense a freedom for a time, and then the difficulty will begin allover again. The question arises –"Wasn't I set free from this?"

Yes. However, your will, and your heart will re-visit areas of pain, with the guidance of the Holy Spirit, always receiving a different point of healing, many times from the same instance or injury. There are also times, when the enemy seeks to re-enslave a person (Matthew 12:43-44)

When the inner house is cleaned, it is important that it be immediately filled with the Word of God, and with the Spirit of God. Habits and practices which the flesh has learned to depend upon must be resisted. (James 4:7) This is called walking in deliverance. **It requires the involvement and empowered battling of your entire being.**

Mourning Prophet

Jeremiah stood on the mountain just outside Jerusalem, weeping.

How could they treat the Father like this? Didn't they see how much He loved them? Didn't they see that they had allowed the seeds of idolatry and evil to grow in the land until they had exhausted Him with their sin? It had begun long ago, in the days of Samuel, when they had asked for a king instead of a Father.

Their weaknesses had given way to captivity.

It was coming soon.

They would lose their nation. They would lose everything, and come under the harsh dictatorship of Nebuchadnezzar, the king of Babylon. It would be seventy years before they would be allowed to return,

        broken,
                destroyed,
                        without hope.

Why had they allowed it to come to this?

They had forgotten His mercy.
        They had neglected His ways.
                They had forsaken His power.

                        They had forgotten His love.

Steps to Healing the Will

It is essential that we understand that it is Satan's strategy, to destroy the human will, and render it helpless. Father God has created mankind with a free will. It is our heavenly Father's will and plan that our human will be developed and nurtured to partner with His plans and designs for our lives.

> **Example:** By the means of free-will, a person can receive or reject salvation in Jesus Christ. God will not violate the human will. He has provided the Gift of His Son, and a decision must be made.

1. Realize that Abba Father God created the human will.

2. The will of man must be healed, just like the heart and conscience.

Will you release trust to your Heavenly Father to heal you? Can you make the choice to trust Him?

_____

_____

3. Healing begins with small steps. Make small decisions. (For example, "I choose to believe that God has a loving, Divine plan, for my entire life.")

What small choices can you make right now?

_____

_____

4. Utilize your will to take a stand with the Word of God, by rejecting the lies of the enemy of your soul. He tells you, "You can't. Helplessness, victimization, and hopelessness are always going to be there." Make a decision to say "Yes, I can, and I will,"

Choose two of the following scriptures to memorize. Philippians 4:13, Isaiah 54:17, Isaiah 54:14, Psalm 103: 10, Psalm 103:13-14, Romans 8:37, Roman~ 8:38-39. When the thoughts and threats of futility come to mind, quote the Word of God in response until they leave. Write out one of the scriptures you have chosen here.

_____

5. Make priority decisions:
    a. to pray (for however small an amount of time, on a consistent basis. It will lengthen as you become stronger).
    b. to praise (every day)
    c. to read the Word of God (even if it is only a verse or two to begin with)
    d. to memorize the Word ("Thy word have I hid in my heart, that I might not sin against Thee." Psalm 119:11)
    e. to fellowship with other believers on a consistent *basis*. Share with trustworthy believers your struggle and desire to grow.

6. Speak out of *your* mouth with boldness and directness your heart for the Lord and the strengthening of your will to serve Him. In this way, you are making a confession of your life's decision to be all that Father God has designed you to be. (From the abundance of the heart, the mouth speaks.)

7. Submit yourself to the Lord on a regular basis.
    a. Your spirit
    b. Your soul (mind, will and emotions)
    c. Your body

The last three points have much to do with your commitment to growth, in everyday relationship with Father God. How can you schedule your time to facilitate this relationship?

_____

_____

"And you shall love the Lord your God with all your heart, with all your soul, and with all your mind, and with all your strength. Luke 12:30

What is Obedience?

"Hereafter, I will not talk (share thoughts) much with you, for the prince of this world cometh and hath nothing in me. But that the world may know that I love the Father, and as the Father gave me commandment, even so I do." John 14:30-31

Definition: To fall into one's place of rank and operate under the authority and direction of another. To be accountable for one's actions. To honor and be loyal in word and action to God-given delegated authorities, whether secular or spiritual.

In the New Testament two words are used for obedience.

"hupakoe" –compliance and submission, heed given to counsels given, obedience.

"hupotasso" –to arrange one's self under (in rank), yielding to advice and counsel, to voluntarily put into subjection, to obey.

1. Jesus obeyed His earthly parents. He is our example.   Luke 2:51
    a. We are subject to our earthly parents for correction.   Hebrews 12:9
    b. We are subject to our heavenly
Father for direction to live our lives.

2. All authorities are put in our lives by the Father.   Romans 13:1-5
    a. We are to obey every authority of man.   Titus 3:1
    b. We are to obey authorities within the church   Hebrews 13:17

3. We are to obey all ordinances of man's authority willingly.   I Peter 2:13

What does Titus 3:1 say? Write it here. _____

_____

4. Employees are to be obedient to their employers,   I Peter 2:18
whether they are gentle, or whether they are harsh.   Colossians 3:22

5. When we obey we will be blessed. When we   Deut.11:27-28
disobey, we will not be blessed, but cursed.   Job 36:11-12

How does Father God consider the choice to obey? Write out I Samuel 15:22 here.

_____

6. The fruit of refusal to obey is a hard heart, rebellion, and bondage. — Nehemiah 9:17

7. All dominions and kingdoms will obey the Father eventually, whether voluntarily or involuntarily. (We have the choice to do it voluntarily now.) — Daniel 7:27

What part of our nature will not voluntarily choose to obey? Write out Romans 8:7 here.

_____

_____

8. When we are under God's authority, we move with His authority, but that is not to be a focal point in our Life-walk. Salvation should be our focal point. — Luke 10:17-20; I Peter 3:22; Mark 1:27

10. Establishing our own standards of righteousness is a counterfeit for obedience to Father God. — Romans 10:3

Write out Romans 10:3 here. _____

_____

11. Submitted hearts create community — I Peter 2:1- 3:5
12. Believers are to submit to one another — Ephesians 5:21
    a. Children are to obey their parents — Ephesians 6:1; Colossians 3:20

What blessing is given to those who honor their parents?

_____

_____

13. An obedient heart loves God entirely. — John 14:15
14. An obedient heart does the will of the Father. — Matthew 7:21
15. An obedient heart will cause a stable life. — Matthew 7:24-27

Where do you want your life to be built?

_____

17. Those who can keep rank are not of double heart   I Chronicles 12:33

In what ways would you like the Holy Spirit to enable you to live with a congruent heart – undivided, loyal and sure of Abba's love and care?

_____

_____

_____

"We will obey the voice of the Lord our God." Jeremiah 42:6

Principle: The desire to show our love for
Abba Father with obedience
Must replace our own desire
To be recognized or followed,
Demanding obedience

(Jesus said), "If you love, keep my commandments." John 14:15

The desire to serve must replace
The desire to be served.

"He who would be the greatest among you, let him be the servant of all. " (Matthew 28: 11)

The Rebuilder

He stood just to the right of the king of Persia. He hadn't slept in days. As he poured the king's wine, his hand shook.

"What's wrong, Nehemiah?" It was a concerned question from a gracious and powerful leader.

"Nothing, sir. I just don't feel well. That's all." Nehemiah looked down at the floor.

"Don't tell me that, good friend. You are sick at heart. I know you. What is troubling you?"

Nehemiah began to share with his master the concerns on his heart. As he did so, Cyrus saw a needy people behind the eyes of Nehemiah. In addition, he saw a chance to restore and help people who were under his care.

Jerusalem's walls had been destroyed seventy years prior, by Nebuchadnezzar of Babylon. The temple had been burned to the ground. The people living there had no protection from enemies or even wild animals. Something would have to be done.

Ezra had already been sent to rebuild the temple. They had needed a spiritual place of peace. That had been reborn.

Now it was time for the walls to be restored. The city needed definition and boundaries as to its personality and heart. Jerusalem. She didn't know who she was. She was broken down.

Cyrus decided to send Nehemiah to rebuild the walls of the city. He would confer upon him a governorship, which included authority to rally troops if need be. That would do it.

Nehemiah, whose name meant Comforter, was the man for the job.

But there would be enemies; Sanballat and Tobiah would fight against the process.

>No matter.
>>Nehemiah would rally the people.

They would build.
They would fight.
They would become strong.

>They would once again become the servants of the Most High God.

What personal discoveries do you see in the Word of God regarding the need to pursue emotional health as a lifestyle? Take time to consider your discoveries, and make notes here.

> Please listen to the twelfth CD, utilizing your notebook, for Session Twelve
>
> "How To Retain Transformation"
> before you move ahead

Notes:

The Principle of Restoration

*"The Lord is my shepherd, I shall not want. He maketh me to lie
down in green pastures; he leadeth me beside the still waters.
He restoreth my soul: he leadeth me in the paths of righteousness
for his name's sake." Psalm 23: 1-3*

"And He (Jesus) entered again into the synagogue; and there was a man there which had a withered hand And they watched him, whether he would heal him on the Sabbath day; that they might accuse him. And he saith unto the man which had the withered hand, 'Stand forth.' And he saith unto them, 'Is it lawful to do good on the Sabbath day, or to do evil? To save life, or to kill?' But they held their peace. And when he had looked round on them with anger, being grieved for the hardness of their hearts, he saith unto the man,

'Stretch forth thine hand.'

And he stretched it out: and his hand was restored whole as the other." " Mark 3: 1-5

The word "withered" is the Greek word "xeros" , which means "shrunk away, wasted, dry (like land without water)."

There are those who, through bondage and addiction, feel as though their entire soul has withered up into nothing. They feel numb, and unable to make sense of those things around them.

It is to those people that Jesus says, in the way only He can,

"Stretch it forth. Just try."

And as you do, moving toward freedom, in whatever-sized steps you can manage, doing all you know to do,

He will meet you.

He will heal you.

He will restore you.

HE IS THE RESURRECTION AND THE LIFE (John 5:28-29)

(Hebrew) "shuwb" –to return again, restore, bring back, to be brought back
(Hebrew) "'alah" –to go up, ascend, rouse or stir (used in regard to restoring physical health) (Hebrew) "shalam" –to pay, to make peace with, to be repaid (used in regard to restoring material possessions)

    1. We can ask to have joy restored.   Psalm 51:12

When we come to the realization of what has been stolen from our lives, and who (the devil) has done the stealing, what does Proverbs 6:31 promise us?

_____

_____

    2. It is possible to be so beaten down
       there is not even a desire for restoration.   Isaiah 42:44
    (Ask the Holy Spirit to kindle the desire within you.)

We ask the Lord to restore our lives, so that as an end result we will be a light to those to don't know Him (to the Gentiles). Write out Isaiah 49:6 here.

_____

_____

    3. The Lord will heal us, and lead us, and restore   Isaiah 57:18
      comfort to those who have mourned over us.

    4. When everyone else considers us to be an outcast,   Jeremiah 30:17
      the Lord says, "I will restore you and heal you."

Write out the promise given to us in Joel 2:25-27.

_____

_____

    5. He has promised to satisfy the longing   Psalm 107:9
      soul and fill the hungry soul with goodness.

What are you asking the Father to restore in your life?

_____

_____

Principles of Spiritual Liberty

1. When we seek the Father's precepts,   Psalm 119:45
we walk in spiritual liberty.

2. Spiritual liberty in Christ must be maintained,   Galatians 5:1
and held on to, or the believer can find himself in   Galatians 2:4
bondage through deception.   II Peter 2:19

In what ways are you determining now to continue to maintain spiritual and emotional life and health after finishing this workbook?

_____

_____

3. The purpose of spiritual liberty is to serve others,   Galatians 5:13
not to give ourselves permission to satisfy   I Peter 2:16
fleshly appetites.

4. The believer who walks in spiritual liberty will   James 1:25
be a doer of the Word of God. (It will become part
of his lifestyle).

In what ways can you choose to serve others in the new places of spiritual and emotional liberty you have discovered during this course?

_____
_____

_____

What actions are you now utilizing and plan to maintain in order to continue this process of growth and wholeness in your life?

_____

_____

5. The reward for maintaining spiritual liberty on earth is the crown of life.   James 1:12
Jude 21

6. When we know Jesus (The Truth --John 14:6), we are made free. (The more we know Him, the more we are free!!)   John 8:32
John 8:36

7. When we render the carnal man as dead ("don't listen to him, he doesn't live here anymore"), Christ lives His Life in us as a vessel.   Galatians 2:20

It is important to realize that our lives in Christ are continually growing, changing and developing. If at any time we cease that development, it should serve as a signal for concern in our hearts.

Are these courses or studies you have in mind to plug this "learning curve" of your heart and life into for further growth? If not, if might be a good idea to shop at a local Christian bookstore for materials that would help you to continue to allow the Holy Spirit to "build" your spiritual and emotional being. If you would like more materials from our ministry, please check out our website at awakenedtogrow.com, or email us at awakenedtogrow@yahoo.com. Blessings!